790.192   F532a   1971
FISH
ACTIVITIES PROGRAM FOR
SENIOR CITIZENS
                    7.95

Activities Program
for
Senior Citizens

ACTIVITIES PROGRAM
FOR
SENIOR CITIZENS

Harriet U. Fish, O. T. R.

PARKER PUBLISHING COMPANY, INC.   WEST NYACK, N.Y.

To my husband Ed, who started this venture
with me, but did not live to see the results

Printed in the United States of America
ISBN 0-13-003590-4
B & P

WHAT THIS BOOK
WILL DO FOR YOU

This book gives you a treasury of proven practical ideas for helping senior citizens live happier and fuller lives. It is designed to help you help men and women in their sunset years gain self respect and initiative. That's why we have predicated the book on the three "grand essentials to happiness" so eloquently expressed by Joseph Addison—"something to do, something to love and something to hope for." Together, these three ingredients spell the difference between a living death and a life worth living for senior citizens.

Most especially this book is a storehouse of plans for professional directors of hospitals, nursing homes, community programs and senior citizens organizations. It is also for the para-professional who wants practical guidelines with which to help senior citizens reaffirm life, rather than accept resignation and defeat. The programs outlined in this book are not just pipe dreams. They are an outgrowth of a sound application of geriatric psychology. Every idea in this book works. Every one is in use today. Thus these ideas are indispensible teaching aids, enabling you to create a dynamic activities program tailored to your needs—structured to help the senior citizens for which you are responsible literally become born again.

Activities Program for Senior Citizens is divided into three sections. Section I provides those necessary practical preliminaries and background needs for setting up, with firm foundation, a program for constructively occupying long hours. It tells you how to organize your program, step-by-step, from an empty room to a fully operational plan of action. It thoroughly covers the subject in terms of who, where, what, how and why.

It tells who should be selected for the job of conducting the activity program, what his qualifications and abilities should be and how to find him.

New ways to incorporate volunteers into your activity program are stressed as well as how to find them, use them and keep them.

It tells you where to locate the "hub" or workroom for the activity program, the desirable physical features, the necessary materials and equipment and the methods for obtaining such acquisitions.

Activities Program for Senior Citizens includes the attitudes and philosophies which should be incorporated into the activity program, and what to do to keep things going in the right direction for them and by them. It emphasizes how to get the elderlies "into the act," to make them want to do, to be, to live.

Common sense ideas to be used in handling groups with special and personality limits are a vital feature of the book.

It tells you what kinds of things you can make in inventions and adaptations of basic equipment for the individual needs and how to use them. These are applicable whether the problems are the result of illness or aging.

Section II covers the adaptations and adjustments necessary in planning parties, entertainments and holiday features for senior citizens. Accented in this section are considerations in selection of foods, decorations and displays for this age group, as well as the adjustment of games, active and sedentary, and other forms of recreation, to the needs and limitations of the elderly.

The importance of the activity program's affect upon the public relations of the facility or organization and its relation to the surrounding community is emphasized.

Section III selects certain handicrafts and skills and then describes how they are adjusted and adapted in degree and technique for use with the older age group. It tells you how to make these necessary adjustments, what basic principles to apply, and gives practical advice, hoping to help you avoid pitfalls.

In the last chapter is additional help, including an extensive bibliography, which is divided according to the three sections of the book.

Sprinkled throughout the book are work simplification ideas and suggestions, with a consideration for the pressures on the Activity Program Director, and thoughts toward making progress as easy and productive as possible.

The "why" of all of this is very real and present today. We have an increasing number of Senior Citizens over 65 years of age in our society. We need to find ways to encourage them to continue to be interested, active, curious and inquisitive, mentally and physically.

The philosophies repeated in this book reflect an understanding and awareness which must be present in order to be a successful Activity Program Director with this age group. Most important in understanding the ways of an oldster is the fact that he is not like a child, that he has experienced life and made decisions. You must put yourself into his shoes, think as he does—thus involve the basic ingredients in operating successful *activities for senior citizens.*

Harriet U. Fish

ACKNOWLEDGEMENTS

The content for *Activities Program for Senior Citizens* has been developed over twenty-five years of working in the field of Occupational Therapy with all ages and kinds of people having many degrees of health problems. Some of this material has been published previously, in a series of articles for NURSING HOMES, the official magazine of the American Nursing Homes Association; TAKE IT EASY, a pamphlet published by the Washington State Heart Association and the American Heart Association; and other professional and college journals. It has, however, been expanded and greatly enlarged.

I wish to express my gratitude to my many friends among Occupational Therapists, Activity Program Directors, Volunteers, Teachers and Librarians whose suggestions, ideas and programs have helped produce these chapters. For the photographs, I wish to thank Mr. John Nelson, of Northwestern Glass Co. in Seattle, a photographer by avocation, an industrial engineer by profession.

For great constructive support and encouragement under trying emotional circumstances, to say nothing of the hours spent typing the final drafts, I wish to say thank you to Helen Carr, of Issaquah, Washington. Without her sincerely given voluntary help, I would never have made the deadline.

My hope is that with the publication and use of this book, many more programs will be developed into meaningful therapeutic and leisure time activities for our Senior Citizens—programs which tell them "Someone still cares about me."

H.U.F.

They may not need me—yet they might
I'll let my heart be just in sight,
A smile so small as mine might be
Precisely their necessity.

Emily Dickinson.

Contents

- Arranging groups according to space limits, mental limits
- Scheduling
- Suggestions for group activities

- How to get them
- How to use them
- How to keep them

- Inventions and adaptations to assist: Stroke victims, oldsters with physical handicaps, the confused, disoriented, and uncoordinated

Section II Parties, Holidays and Other Entertainment

- Includes ideas for use of volunteers and outside help; especially important in this part of the Activity Program

- The open house
- Festive holidays
- Fun and games—active
- Fun and games—sedentary and socializing

Section III Creative Handicraft Projects

- Limits of scale, complexity and color
- How to keep projects simple and easy to see
- Uses for finished work

- Simple forms from clay
- Beads, tiles and mosaics
- Where to get materials
- Recipes for artificial clay

- Machines, types and uses
- Other equipment
- Embroidery
- Turkish knotting frame

- Looms, types and uses
- Materials
- Uses for woven cloth

- How to get and use them

- Men are difficult to motivate
- Woodworking
- Whittling
- Rock tumbling

- Stationary and animated
- Newsletters

- Where to buy materials and equipment
- Where to find patterns
- General sources of information and advice
- Bibliography

Activities Program
for
Senior Citizens

Section I

KEY ELEMENTS OF
SUCCESSFUL ORGANIZATION

Chapter 1

PLANNING THE DYNAMIC PROGRAM

Before we can talk intelligently about organization, we must know what we are organizing for. What is an activity program for senior citizens?

An activity program for senior citizens is anything and everything which offers participation and self-activation to a group of elderly people and the staff around them. A good activity program makes a group "swing." It creates happy faces; and it makes everyone involved—those who pay, those who are paid, and those who watch from the outside—glad that the group is together.

An activity program for senior citizens is not a neatly typed schedule of events filling each day, and it is not rows of shiny tools waiting in a spacious shop for someone to use them. It is not even a bustling staff of well-meaning volunteers carrying busy-work to and fro. Any activity program for senior citizens must be organized to motivate those citizens to use whatever time, energy, and attention they are able to apply, for their own pleasure and benefit.

It is the purpose of this chapter, therefore, to tell how a program can set up an organizational base from which leverage, motion and swing can be created for the benefit of senior citizens and the people who serve them.

BUILDING THE FRAME

Any activity program for senior citizens—whether it is in a nursing care facility, retirement home, community recreation program, or senior citizens club—is part of a larger organization. As in any organization, its director must receive authority, backing, support, and leadership from the top administrator. (See Figure 1-1)

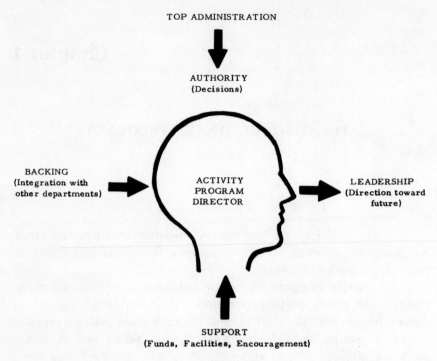

Figure 1-1

Building the organizational frame for a worthwhile and permanent activities program takes time, because the Activity Program Director and the Administrator must agree on a number of things in order to be assured that the authority, backing, support, and leadership will have a solid basis. That is why the Activity Program Director should be a paid member of the staff. An unpaid volunteer can seldom be depended upon to give full-scale attention to the job of developing and operating a permanent program; and, he almost certainly will not feel the necessary compulsion to stay within the organizational frame. This is true especially as regards recognizing the authority and leadership of the Administrator. Volunteers definitely have a place as assistants to the Activity Program Director, but they should not be counted upon to direct any program which is intended to be a long-term, productive part of the organization.

A paid, professional Activity Program Director will carefully relate his ability and experience to the Administrator's knowledge of the kind of program the facility needs.

What Is the Activity Program Director Expected to Do ?   (Now or in the Future)

- Instruct individual and group crafts?
- Organize and direct patient entertainment and recreation? (Such as, parties, musicales, movies, and discussion groups)
- Socialize with patients during working hours by playing cards, watching TV, or "just visiting"?
- Recruit, train, and direct volunteers?
    - —to assist with entertainment and recreation
    - —to keep patients company
    - —to provide transportation and errand service for patients
    - —to mend clothes, prepare party food, make table favors
- Keep records and make reports?
    - —of patient contact time and progress
    - —of volunteer time and services
    - —of income and expense
- Publish a newsletter?
- Organize and direct employee parties?
- Participate in public relations effort?
    - —by organizing open house days
    - —by lecturing to community or professional groups
    - —by conducting tour groups through the facility
    - —by writing news releases about activities

What Facilities and Services Will the Management Provide?

- An activity room?
    - —locked during off-use hours, or open around the clock?
    - —occupied during off-use hours by food service, meetings, exercise class, or equipment storage?
- Use of other rooms for special activities?
    - —Dining room for bingo, church, movies
    - —Lounge room for teas, discussion groups
    - —Conference room for interviews, volunteer training classes
- Transportation of patients to and from activities within the building?
    - —by nursing staff or aides
    - —by other patients
- Adequate locked storage area for materials, equipment, and display props?
- Office equipment, such as, desk, file cabinet, typewriter, telephone?

- Gifts, lunches, or other gratuities for volunteers?
- Money to start and operate the program, such as:
    —initial investment for material and equipment
    —monthly petty cash fund
- Liability insurance under the institution's blanket policy?

Hours of Work

- Full or part-time?
- Daily or weekly schedule?
- Daily work period? (Depends on patient care routine—baths, doctor's calls, hairdresser, meals, etc.)
- Rest periods?
    —in work area or in employees' room?
- Off-premises time?—
    —for purchasing and preparation of projects
    —for volunteer recruiting and public relations work
    —for observing activity programs in other institutions
- Flexible work schedule to substitute weekend or evening work on special events for regularly scheduled work time?

Amount and Method of Payment

- How much?
- Hourly rate, or salary?
- Paid weekly, semi-monthly, or monthly?
- Additional payment for extra work on special events?
- Fringe benefits such as medical insurance, disability insurance, life insurance, pension, profit-sharing, year-end bonus?
- Time clock, weekly time sheet, or honor system for recording hours worked?

Other Conditions

- Uniform, or other special clothing?
- Smoking rules?
- How to communicate with other staff members?
    —attend staff meetings?
    —mail box in central office?
    —scheduled daily or weekly conferences with individuals?

Some difference of opinion exists as to whether the results of this discussion should be recorded in an employment contract. Although a formal written agreement may provide some degree of

messenger when your job is to be where the patient action is.
Another good use for the central message system: to seek and receive
advice from staff members whose skill in their professions can help
you in yours.

Have a place for everything. Keep tools, materials, supplies, and
equipment in specific places so that you and your helpers can find an
item and put it to use without making patients wait and fret.
Consider where you would naturally go for each type of item, as well
as where someone else would naturally look for it in your absence.
Make a final arrangement so that your helpers will be able to work
just as smoothly as you do, on the days when you are not around or
when you don't want to be interrupted. Paint, brushes, and wiping
rags, for instance, will be in one cabinet or locker. Needles, scissors,
elastic tape, and thread will be in a box or on a Lazy Susan which
can be set on a table and then stored away in one easy operation at
the end of the day.

Another essential for good organization of articles is labeling.
Containers, cupboard doors, desk drawers, even the shelves in open
storage areas, should be identified.

Keep work spaces and storage areas picked up. Senior citizens
often strew things around and then forget where they left them; part
of an Activity Program Director's job is to compensate for ailing
memories. End each day or work period by gathering, sorting, and
replacing all of the bits and pieces on the tables and floor. You will
find quite a bit of gear in your own pockets, also, if you have
efficiently tucked away small pick-ups on the run during the day.

Maintain an adequate business center for yourself, in or close to
the activity room, with your own chair, desk, record storage, and
telephone.

Organize a personalized filing method. Use it to hold and feed
out all phone numbers, addresses, dates, names, reminders and ideas
which you need to keep things moving every day.

An Activity Program Director's information file is usually in
two parts: a resource listing, and a collection of reference material. A
box file for 3"x5" cards, arranged according to the way your
particular mind works, does well for the resource file. For example:

- Birthday Cakes (bakeries, caterers)
- Services for the Blind (talking book library, Braille publications, Sight
  and Hearing Association)
- Church Volunteers (local ministerial association, & helpers)
- Cookie Recipes (sugar-free, for diabetic patients)

- Donated Supplies (clothing manufacturers, lumber yards)
- Films and Slides (libraries, airlines, tape clubs)
- Ideas (on the fire, ready to start, started)
- Music (schools, churches, community band, individuals)
- Potential Staff (summer workers, part-time specialists)
- Volunteers (for errands, typing, at-home project preparation, bingo)

The reference file, usually in a file cabinet or large desk drawer, organizes such material as:

Patterns	Mimeo stencils
Catalogues	Clipping file (pictures & designs)
Instruction manuals	Financial records
Forms	Personnel & Volunteer records
Newsletter copies	Magazines

In addition, a personal file folder should be kept for the items which do not fit into any of the regular categories.

A couple of files like this, kept up to date with a few minutes work each day, will give you and your assistants all of the information you need and will probably earn you the reputation of having many of the answers to other people's questions as well.

Select clothing suitable to the conditions of your work. Colored blouse and skirt combinations are changeable, efficient, and distinctive, in contrast to the medical staff's white uniforms. Pockets must accommodate scissors, pencil, keys, Band-Aids, notebook, and tissue for wiping up spills. Street clothes are all right, too, if they are comfortable and practical, and if you can wear a smock over them when you are painting things or running the mimeograph. If you normally wear a uniform or a standard outfit, use street clothes for a change of pace at an evening event or on a bright spring day—you'll be surprised at the effect on the patients.

Prepare to supervise. This refers to both the paid and volunteer helpers. Be sure that each person has a specific job, understands what it is, and recognizes his responsibilities to you and to the patients; then, provide firm guidance to mold each helper into your way of doing things. And don't overlook the importance of a regular evaluation of each person's contribution to the program, for his benefit and yours.

Set up systematic communications within your group to minimize interruptions, and to enable others to carry on when you are absent. A file folder for each helper, in the reference file, will contain written material, and frequent personal conferences will provide a time during which items can be discussed. The written communications will explain the house rules, stress the importance of regular attendance, define appropriate clothing, and discuss treatment of confidential patient information.

Records

A good Activity Program Director should be occupied with people, not with paper, but some record-keeping is necessary. The important thing is to reduce the paperwork to its essentials. Maintain only the records you need to keep track of patient contact, staff hours, personnel data, major equipment inventory, expenses and income, and activity schedules. Your employer may have additional requirements which must be met, and these will vary between institutions, but other than that, the major records described in this section will do the job.

All you really need to work with is a properly designed desk book, a couple of wall calendars with squares to write in, your 3"x5" card file, and a set of personnel folders in the reference file. Sounds almost too simple, doesn't it? But it works.

The desk book is the heart of the system. The best one we've found is the *Daytimer,* which you can buy from Daytimers, Inc., P.O. Box 1728, Allentown, Pennsylvania, 18105. Pages for each day provide for an hour-by-hour listing of patient contacts, daily time record of each staff member, and lists of things to be accomplished or followed up. A special page in each month's section, specifically designed as a money record, helps you prepare cash statements as well.

The wall calendars serve two purposes. One is a combination sign-up sheet and attendance record for volunteers; the other records upcoming activities for patients and department personnel. File the old calendar sheets for a complete record of what has been going on, and when. You also have a ready record of volunteer hours on which to base service awards.

Equipment inventory is kept on a set of 3"x5" cards in the resource file. The file needn't be extensive, just include the large items such as power tools, looms, sewing machines, rock tumblers, etc. Each equipment card should show the date of acquisition, description of the item, serial number, and source.

Accurate sales and money records are necessary if the activity department is organized on an "items for sale" basis. If the volume of business is not large, the money record in your *Daytimer* will hold all the information about products delivered and money received. If the business office will not do the collecting for you (which is by far the best way to handle a small sales volume), your delivery record should be matched regularly against the office's receipt slips which come to you via your clipboard.

You may feel that you need more detail than is included in our suggestions. If so, seek advice from those who know about these things—your employer's accountant, a patient or resident who has had business experience, or the reference service of your local library. No record system is universally applicable, and you will undoubtedly want to shorten and simplify whatever method is recommended, in order to meet your objective of working with people, not with paper.

Finances

A properly conducted activity program will often be able to finance its own materials and supplies through sales revenues and donations, but it will never pay back the investment required to house, equip, and staff it. Activity programs are not intended to pay off in money. They are expected to generate goodwill, happiness, self-realization; all of the things which senior citizens badly need and upon which the institution's attractiveness depends. The money which is put out to start and maintain such an activity program is, therefore, an investment in intangibles, and will probably be held to a minimum by the management until the program has thoroughly proven itself.

You do not need a great deal of money to involve a large proportion of your facility's residents in beneficial activities if you concentrate on the parts of the program which are needed first, and on the minimum requirements to start these parts. Ability to keep investment and operating costs down, while increasing patient participation and general goodwill, is the real measure of an Activity Program Director's success.

These ideas will help you plan and regulate your spending for maximum mileage:

(1) Make sure that you and the Administrator agree on how much will be invested in equipment and supplies to start or expand the program, and then make sure that you stay within those limits.

(2) Decide with the Administrator on a maximum limit for any single outlay, beyond which you will consult before going ahead.

(3) Agree on how to account for outside contributions of money or major equipment. Will they be deducted from the original budget, or can you take them as extras and use them as you see fit?

(4) Spend the initial funds carefully, as needs become apparent. If most of your program participants are women, you can be pretty sure that sewing, mending, and minor crafts, will be popular. You will want to buy basic equipment for these needs. When later expansion of the program develops interest in larger projects, you can consider investing in a small loom, a treadle sewing machine, and some basic woodworking hand tools for the men.

(5) Maintain a minimum petty cash account for purchase of everyday needs. Expenses of this type for a 100-150 bed nursing home, for example, will average about $25.00 per month. Record each expenditure in your desk book so that you can submit an accurate, businesslike accounting along with your request for replenishment of the fund.

(6) Develop, as early as possible, sources of volunteer help and donated materials from the outside community. This is important, because if you have to buy or hire all of the goods and talent for your program you will have a difficult time making ends meet on the kind of a budget to which a non-profit department is usually restricted. It is so important, in fact, that two other chapters in this book are devoted to these subjects.

Purchasing

Organizing the procurement of materials and equipment which your department uses is closely related to financial management of the activity program. You should, therefore, try to do a large part of the buying yourself, especially at the start. Most Activity Program Directors prefer to do their own purchasing a little bit at a time; partly because of the specialized nature of their requirements, but mostly because they do not have the space or money to buy or store large quantities in advance of use. This does not mean that you must do the shopping yourself. A properly instructed volunteer shopper can do it for you once you have determined what quality you want and how much you will pay for it.

Group purchasing with other departments or with other organizations similar to yours may also be economical. You might save quite a bit of time and money, for example, by getting together with:

- The Housekeeping Department, for twill tape, canvas, rubber yardage, unbleached sheeting.
- The Maintenance Department, for tools, woodworking supplies, lumber, hardware, and paint.
- Other nearby institutions, for cloth yardage, warping cotton, Belfast cord, and other items normally available only in large quantities.

Some employers require that all purchases be made through a central office; in which case it is especially important to make sure that your purchase requisitions describe clearly what it is you want and how much you expect to be charged for it.

Whichever way you do your purchasing—individually, by volunteers, as part of a cooperative group, or through a central office—insist on good quality. Be sure you have the best, even though it means having less quantity from a limited budget. An Activity Program Director who is responsible for the effective use of tools and equipment by elderly, ill, or emotionally stressed people simply cannot afford to have equipment breakdowns or material failures magnify his patients' infirmities.

Another point about quality and usefulness: avoid buying packaged craft kits. Kits are expensive. They often include materials which you already have, and they are difficult to adapt to the limitations of the aged. Develop your own project kits instead, from general purpose material and tools which you have purchased at more reasonable prices.

Set aside a special time each week for purchasing, during which you will concentrate on the telephoning, shopping, and record-keeping it requires. Keep a notepad handy at your desk to list the items you need. You will save as much as two hours a week by doing all the business at once.

Record the serial number and specifications of each major item of equipment and file the operating instructions where you can find them quickly. Using an electric vibrating marker identify all tools and machinery, large and small, as property of your department, so that they can be retrieved from patients' rooms or the maintenance shop without argument.

Do not hesitate to shop around for good prices, consistent with the quality which you require. A nearby hardware or dry goods store which knows your institution should, in return for a major share of your purchasing, grant an appreciable reduction from list price and make a special effort to stock the items you need. Don't buy when you can beg. Waste materials obtained free from other departments of your facility can be used in place of purchased supplies for many projects. They will produce a copious flow of such useful items as:

- Ends of wood, partially used cans of paint, and scraps of styrofoam from the maintenance shop
- Empty pill bottles, plastic syringe (tubes), and exposed X-ray film from the medical department
- Plastic bleach jugs from the laundry

- Cartons, large metal cans, paper food containers of all sizes and shapes, and many cups of coffee from the kitchen
- Adding machine tape, plastic tape reels, and short pencils (to fit into your pocket without catching onto things) from the business office

Procurement of all the material things which a good activity program requires can be a demanding chore if not properly organized. Only your continuous insistence on top-quality, trouble free equipment and supplies; careful organization of your shopping and record-keeping time; and a receptive attitude toward other peoples' surpluses will keep it from being a distracting burden.

Volunteers and Donations

These final two sections of the activity program organization diagram are in several ways the most important of all. Happy and appreciated volunteers are the best possible recruiters of additional help for your program and of new patients for your facility; a steady flow of donated items will stretch your budget and provide materials and tools you might not otherwise be able to afford.

You must organize for this kind of help; it definitely does not appear by itself.

Summary

The success of any activity program is in direct proportion to the amount of time which its director and staff are able to spend with the people whom the program is intended to serve. Proper organization of the program will maximize this time, and will provide the facilities, outside help, and inside support to make it effective and permanent.

Only if you surround yourself with a suitable framework of authority, *to provide good management decisions relating your experience to the kind of program which the facility needs;* backing, *to equate importance of the activity program with other parts of the organization;* support, *to provide adequate funds, working areas, and an encouraging word when the going is rough; and* leadership, *to point out new paths of service as the institution expands, and effectively arrange the way you do things within your department, will you be properly ready to help your patients use the time, energy, and care which they have available for their own pleasure and benefit.*

Chapter 2

SELECTING AN
EFFECTIVE ACTIVITY
PROGRAM DIRECTOR

If you are the administrator of an organization which serves senior citizens, this chapter is for you; you are the one who must decide whether or not to encourage and support an activity program for your residents. You must pick the right person to make it go.

Suppose that your busy day of management duties has been interrupted by a phone conversation with a patient's daughter, who wants to arrange a special birthday party for the 92-year-old. (Her call came while you were reading the local minister's letter about bringing the church choir for a Sunday afternoon concert.) At the same time, several dozen residents are wheel-chairing aimlessly through the halls and complaining about the weather because they haven't anything else to do. A couple of men are trying to get up a cribbage game and can't find the equipment, which used to be at the front desk but disappeared last week. As soon as you get off the phone you must interview the lady from the Swedish Club about transporting twenty-five of your loyal Scandinavians to the annual meatball dinner. Does it bother you that no one on the staff has the time or the inclination to help take care of these things? Do you wish you had some sort of an activity program to ensure that everyone has something to do which will make each day different from the one before?

Activity programs, and the people to direct them, are available to do all of these things. You need only decide that a good activity program will show a profit (either in money, if that is your business, or in human benefit if your purpose is purely charitable) by improving the overall quality of whatever job your organization is trying to do. Your choice of action will then depend upon what kind of program you want and what kind of establishment you are operating.

ACTIVITY PROGRAM-WHAT TYPE?

A health care facility, which caters to short-term rehabilitative patients (strokes, fracture cases, cardiacs, and recent amputees), needs an activity program to complement the medical treatment of physical and psychological problems. Longer-term ambulatory and custodial care, on the other hand, requires emphasis on motivation, renewal of lost or forgotten skills, and restoration of self-respect which is often badly damaged when patients are removed more or less permanently from their original home surroundings.

Residents of retirement homes, members of senior citizens' recreation groups, and participants in community programs designed for "going concern" are yet another situation. These senior citizens want leadership, not treatment or motivation. Active and alert, they call for an activity leader who can direct eager learners into new skills and mental experiences which will make an already interesting life more exciting. This type of program usually employs a recreation specialist skilled in organization and leadership of energetic groups, rather than in therapeutic help to ill and infirm individuals.

Development of an activity program for a health care facility is by far the most difficult of the above situations, because it requires application of medical and psychological knowledge, handicraft, recreation, and entertainment skills. Selection of the director for such a program is likewise not any easy matter; the right combination of clinical and craft expertise comes only from proper training and experience.

ACTIVITY PROGRAM DIRECTOR-WHO?

Properly directed activities to improve the physical and mental condition of the aged are the particular province of the trained occupational therapist, as contrasted with the "craft lady" or "recreation leader" approach. The American Occupation Therapy

Association presently defines its profession as, "the art and science of directing man's response to selected activity to promote and maintain health, to prevent disability, to evaluate behavior, and to treat or train patients with physical or psycho-social dysfunction." An older and more concise statement describes the process as one of "utilizing activity, mental or physical, which has been prescribed by a physician, and is guided by the therapist to aid in the recovery from disease, injury, or disability." Both of these definitions emphasize the knowledgeable application of selected activity to improve the condition of medical patients by a person skilled in directing all kinds of activities.

Why, then, shouldn't every senior citizen health care establishment have an O.T.R. (Registered Occupational Therapist) as its activity program director? There are several reasons. Cost is one. Most nursing homes, convalescent hospitals, or rest homes, do not feel that they can afford the salary of such a professionally trained individual to provide a service which is essentially non-billable. Another reason is that many O.T.R.'s have been heavily trained in the techniques of one-to-one treatment of young, individual patients, and do not find a challenge in applying their knowledge to the wider-ranging problems of rehabilitating groups of elderly people to a new kind of institutional life. We do not mean that professional occupational therapy is not being applied to the field of geriatric care; it is, and has been for many years. What we do mean is that too few O.T.R.'s are equipping themselves to supervise medically oriented, wide-scope activity direction which senior citizens' health care facilities can afford.

It seems to us that administrators can greatly improve the quality of health care service available to senior citizens if they will realize the importance of incorporating medical considerations into activity programs which are directed to the particular needs and disabilities of the aged. Take, for example, the senile male patient kept in emotional balance by medication. What happens when his dosage is discontinued for a couple of weeks in order to reduce side effects, and he becomes abusive and uncooperative? Should he simply be shoved into a corner and forgotten, or can a properly trained worker appraise the drop in his tolerance level and provide suitable lower grade activity temporarily? And what about the kindly little lady with arthritic hands and holes in her memory? Does she sit all day in the hall, clumsily balling up her lap robe, or will someone see that she spends at least part of the day in the activity room straightening out stiff fingers by winding yarn into balls?

The untrained person, not knowing what to do in these cases, will, at best, be discouraged and give up. At worst, he may force the patient into improper exertion which may cause physical or psychological damage. On the other hand, a professionally trained or supervised activity director will neither give up nor make damaging mistakes. He will convert patient problems into opportunities for service by fitting activity (mental or physical, individual or group), to the time, energy, and attention which his patients are able to apply.

An activity program conducted or supervised by an occupational therapist can also upgrade the quality and competitive strength of a health care facility in ways other than those illustrated above.

1. The O.T.R. is qualified to provide specific individual therapy, coordinated with the overall activities program which would otherwise not be available. Perceptive motor tests for stroke patients (given unobtrusively on the way to a Wednesday night movie in the lounge room); construction of built-up grips on tools or tableware to bring use back to crippled hands; assignment of the daily mail distribution to a woman leg amputee who must build up arm muscles for her future life in a wheelchair; design and implementation of resting and cock-up splints for the paralyzed extremity; are some of the plus items in the facility's favor which may be accomplished while the therapist is also supervising a group of workers around the activity table.
2. The O.T.R. can meet with the patient's family, as an official representative of the facility, in discussion of patient problems and progress (subject to the authority of the attending physician and the facility's administrator), to suggest ways in which family and friends can support the patient's improvement.
3. The O.T.R.'s professional status and well-rounded knowledge of what his employer's organization is trying to accomplish is admirably suited for public relations work with professional associations and community groups; a function which directly affects patient load and operating profit.

How can a nursing home or other health care facility apply the advantages of a Registered Occupational Therapist's special training and medical background to its activity program at a cost it can afford? We have seen the problem worked out in several ways.

A small organization, or even a large one with a high proportion of ambulatory, custodial patients, can retain an O.T.R. consultant to supervise its activity program director for a certain number of hours or days each month. If the organization employs a properly competent activity director, advice from such a consultant can provide at least a minimum amount of individual therapy to those patients who can best use it.

Or, a C.O.T.A. (Certified Occupational Therapy Assistant)

graduate of an accredited training course may be employed as activity director, again under the supervision of an O.T.R. consultant, to bring a higher level of physiological and psychological awareness into the program at considerably less salary cost than for a full time O.T.R.

In some areas an O.T.R. Consultant from the local state health department is available to facilities for initial development. She may also train activity program directors for eight to ten weeks in the basic needs, values and media for work with the geriatric patient. If you, as an administrator, decide that your needs point to a less highly trained person to operate your activity program, then this may be a source of help to you.

You may find yourself completely on your own, with none of these levels of workers available to you. In this case these suggestions should help in selecting the right person for your particular needs.

ACTIVITY PROGRAM DIRECTOR–REQUIREMENTS?

The development of a general activity and recreational program in a health care facility should be placed in the hands of an Activity Program Director. Employed by the health care facility or institution, he would be in charge of planning and conducting a broad program designed to meet the specialized needs of all individuals, of any age, who may or may not have health problems. Included would be organized activities, such as, crafts, recreational, social, religious, and educational work and fun. These would be planned to encourage individual and group participation, and should provide an atmosphere of mental and physical stimulation and motivational balance.

The number and type of personnel for conducting such an activity program will vary with the size of the facility, its' needs and the objectives of the program, as set down by the Administrator and professional staff. The Activity Program Director may be hired on a full time or part-time basis. Regardless of his training or experience, there are personal qualities necessary in order for the program to be effective.

Qualities to look for are:

- Happy, outgoing and extroverted
- Greater interest in others than in herself
- Personal stability
- Ease in meeting strangers
- Creativity and ingenuity

- Ability to establish a good working arrangement with the community, senior citizens, staff, and volunteers
- Ability to accept and understand health limitations, illness and handicaps in others
- Familiarity with handicrafts, skills, games, and other activities
- Willingness to learn new skills and to accept new ideas
- Good organizational abilities to start and keep things rolling
- Ability to accept responsibility and use it effectively
- Ability to work independently

This important person needs to have a flexible approach to his work, capable of changing, on a moment's notice, his carefully laid plans, at the same time keeping things going smoothly in the right direction. All this must be done with an orderly approach to the work process.

A familiarity with the community outside of the facility is essential. Contact with clubs and groups, knowledge of sources of materials and local services will add to the success of the program. Support for the program from the senior citizen's family and the staff will gain continuity of purpose.

The Activity Program Director must be in good health, have vitality and stamina, be forthright and dependable, and, above all, understand what is expected of him. It is the Administrator's responsibility to make this clear from the start.

ACTIVITY PROGRAM DIRECTOR NEED
FOR GUIDANCE AND LEADERSHIP

A word to the Administrator about providing guidance and leadership. You are adding this person to your staff to bring a spark, to make your facility outstanding in consideration toward your senior citizens' lives and living. He or she can become an invaluable employee and asset if you, as his leader, establish from the start an attitude of confidence and support, which radiates to all levels of employees. The Activity Program Director must establish his own rapport with the aged, families, and employees, but you, in your capacity as policy and decision maker, can give this person the right foundation on which to build a stable and beneficial program. The results of this type of program can make your job easier by having happier, more well-adjusted senior citizens, relaxed and pleased families, and full beds in your facility. Give your Activity Program Director your undivided support and a relative position on your staff which will give him the opportunity to be on a par with other department heads. It is your responsibility to be sure all department heads understand the level of the Activity Program Director's position. Suggestions for effecting this understanding are to include the Acitivity Program Director in the weekly staff meetings, and to add his name to the inter-facility communications.

ACTIVITY PROGRAM DIRECTOR—WHERE TO FIND HER?

Where will you find the right person? The following lists those artisans we consider capable of filling your needs.

1. *Registered Occupational Therapist*—full time or part-time staff member, or in a weekly supervisory or consulting capacity.

    Contact: American Occupational Therapy Association.
    251 Park Avenue South
    New York, N.Y., 10010

    Local Association contacts can be secured from them.

    State Health Department Occupational Therapy Consultant, who may know of available personnel.

    Local or regional universities and community colleges, where occupational therapists are trained.

2. *Certified Occupational Therapy Assistants* (All should be accredited by the American Occupational Therapy Association.)—Full time or part-time employment with a minimum of weekly supervision of a consulting Registered Occupational Therapist.

    Contact: American Occupational Therapy Association
    251 Park Avenue South
    New York, N.Y., 10010

    Local Association contacts can be secured from them.

    Local or regional training centers, such as community colleges.

    State Health Department Occupational Therapy Consultant.

3. *Recreation Specialist*—full time or part-time staff member.

    Contact: National Recreation & Park Association
    1700 Pennsylvania Avenue
    Washington, D.C., 20006

    City, County, & State Recreation and Park Departments.

    Training centers in local universities and colleges.

4. *Activity Program Director*—Not necessarily highly trained, but capable, with some non-professional status and experience.) Full time or part-time.

    Contact: State Health Department Occupational Therapy Consultant.

    Local Hospital Volunteer Directors.

    Park & Recreation Centers.

    Retired teachers.

    Directors of local nursing homes and Retirement Associations.

    Advertisement in organization newsletters or local newspapers.

5. *Volunteer Supervisor*—non-professional status as staff member, full time or part-time employment.

Contact: Local Hospital Volunteer Directors.

Park & Recreation Centers.

Directors of local nursing homes and Retirement Associations.

> "It's the song ye sing
> and the smile ye wear
>
> That's a-makin'
> the sunshine everywhere."
>
> James W. Riley

Summary

Ten Tips for the Administrator

1. *Decide what kind of a program you want, and what results you desire from an Activity Program Director.*
2. *Select the kind of person to fit your needs. Be sure he knows your needs and what you expect of him.*
3. *Give him your support from the start. Become involved in the activity program.*
4. *Include him in the staff. Establish the Activity Program Director's position in a relative place with other department heads. Be sure other department heads understand this.*
5. *Give constructive leadership and guidance when needed; otherwise, let the Activity Program Director carry out his program without interference.*
6. *Make yourself available to the Activity Program Director either at a regularly appointed time, or have an easy arrangement of consultation when he needs your help. Note exchange system is basically good.*
7. *Establish permanent communication channels between all department heads and yourself. Exercise them regularly. Centrally located clip boards or cubbyholes are useful.*
8. *Provide financial remuneration for the kind of job you expect to have done.*
9. *Encourage the Activity Program Director to become a long term employee. In this way you reap the most benefit from your efforts.*
10. *Know what is going on in the activity room.*

Chapter 3

HOW TO DETERMINE
THE PHYSICAL
REQUIREMENTS

An activity program must have a central office of its own. Space, equipment, and materials are major considerations when planning an area from which the total program can function. These requirements must be faced by the Administrator and the Activity Program Director, in a straightforward manner. Plan for expansion of program and addition of personnel from the beginning.

If this department radiates a "welcome mat" atmosphere to everyone, the Activity Program Director will not be the only one centralized there. Consultants and special personnel (such as department aides, O.T.R. consultants, speech therapists, volunteers, and other specialists) as well as regular staff, families and visitors will find this area useful, attractive, and will be in and out, thus needing space for their functions. They will enjoy just standing around and watching the 96 year old man weaving on a round bird-cage loom, or the special look of a current stuffed toy, or asking, "What goes on today?" Think BIG! This is long range planning.

Is this area to be open for use all of the time, even when the director is not there? If so, provide an area in which to lock up expensive equipment, materials, and those tools which could be dangerous to use without supervision. Perhaps the office could be locked and the rest of the room left open. If the library service and game area are housed in the activity room it should be available at all times; some people may like to use the room other than the designated hours when the director is present.

We have found that men and women do not like to work in the same immediate area or at the same table. It is an unusual man who will wheel his chair up to the table among the women and be accepted as one of them. We've had it happen, but we've also had men refuse to even "give a try" in the same area. We suggest you give the men a work space of their own and define it by book shelves, half-high storage shelves, or loom area, so that they feel it is their own personal spot. This partial separation seems to satisfy both groups, and provides easy supervision by one person. One point to keep in mind is this—don't separate the men and women from interest and help in each other's project and progress. Keep them working together in ideas and small helpful things. What man would not be gallant enough to help remove a bottle cover, or open the glue spout? And what woman would not welcome the chance to mend a rip or replace a button? And the men love to eat the special cookies the women whipped up this morning. Admiration of one's work by the opposite sex is stimulation of the highest degree.

Since occupational therapy departments and activity areas have gained status and importance, they have now been moved out of the basement, where adequate space was no problem. With this elevation in importance, and location, we must be compact and efficient in our space usage.

Figure 3-1 shows a flexible floor plan. It will easily house 20-25 people at one time. It also provides the necessary storage and floor space, as stated in the following list of considerations:

The following recommendations are considered to be optimum. It must be stated that very fine programs are being operated in much less well-equipped and designed settings.

1. *Work Area or Room:*

    Shape: generally rectangular, not long and narrow or square, but with a 3' x 4' space relationship. 36 square feet per person minimum including that for equipment.

    Bathroon: should be adjoining and of adequate size to accommodate wheelchairs. Exhaust fan should be installed inside the bathroom. If this facility is not handy to the workroom and activity area, the elderly people with bladder or bowel problems may refuse to take part in activities and not even come to see what is going on.

    Doors: two to the corridor. One to outside and to bathroom should be 3'6" wide.

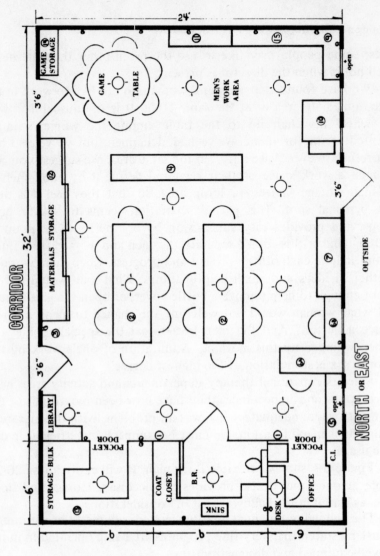

1. Bulletin Board Areas

2. Work Tables and Arm Chairs

3. Walker and Wheel chair storage. Display shelves above

4. Movable Project Storage Shelves on Casters, 36" high. (Used as divider)

5. Ironing Board and Iron

6. Sewing Machines. 6A Treadle, 6B Electric Portable

7. Table Loom Storage and Weaving Supplies

8. Office, standard 2'6" pocket door, with provision for locking Desk, file cabinet

9. Exhaust Fan

10. Floor Loom location, can be turned to operate from any side.

11. 31" high work area for men wheel chair users

12. Materials Storage Cupboard, 4 sliding doors

13. Bulk Storage Room. Standard 2'6" door with lock. Open shelf storage

14. Games storage. Display shelves above

15. Regulation Height Workbench for standing

Figure 3-1

42

Open Areas: keep available for wheelchairs and walkers. Storing and maneuvering takes a great deal of space.

2. *Location and Accessibility of Work Area or Room:*

Centrally located in relation to residents' rooms. Additional convenience is provided by closeness to offices and kitchen.

Preferable to have one outside wall, north or east.

Two doors to corridor, could be one for men and one for women; but regardless, two are needed for wheelchairs and sheer numbers of people coming and going.

On one level, with ramp or elevator available from other floors.

3. *Storage:*

The size and shape of the storage space can have large influence on the variety and type of projects one may offer to the elderly. Small storage provides materials for small projects, which, in general, are not the best for older hands, eyes, and patience.

a. **Storage within the Work Room**: should be 10 cubic ft. per person.

Cupboards: 18" deep shelves minimum; 24" preferred.

Adjustable shelf stripping for maximum use of shelf area.

Magnetic catches are quiet. Repetitive noises can be nerve-wracking to elderly people.

Swing-out doors versus sliding doors (pocket): Swing-out doors take up floor space but offer storage space on inner side. Sliding doors do not take up floor space to open, do not allow for all doors to be open at once, and provide no inner surface storage.

One locked cupboard for sharp tools and poisons.

Cupboard and shelves in the *bathroom.*

Drawers designed for use, at least 3" deep.

b. **Bulk Storage Area**: 18 cubic ft. per person. Separate closed area, as close to the activity room as possible.

Provide a counter for sorting and organizing donated materials. Open shelves on all walls of room, adjustable and utilizing maximum height of wall space.

c. **Fire-proof Cupboard**: An old refrigerator can be used for storage of paints and volatiles.

4. *Ventilation and Heat:*

Temperature should be controlled at 70-75 degrees.

Exhaust fan should be located in the paint and woodworking area to remove odors and dust.

General air ventilation system is necessary. When you have even 10 people in one room, the air needs to be regularly refreshed and replenished.

5. *Windows:*

One wall should have windows, either north or east side. This will leave the three other walls for equipment and cupboards. Curtains and/or blinds provide glare control.

At least two windows should open.

6. *Floors:*

Durable, and waxed with non-skid wax, for ease in wiping up spots.

For cleanliness and ease in mopping, the surface should have a minimum of cracks and joints where dirt can collect.

7. *Acoustics:*

There should be sound control by use of acoustical tile on the ceiling. Noise can be tiring and irritating. Acoustical tile is essential in the men's work area, at least.

8. *Lighting and Electricity:*

Illumination should be provided in general lighting from the ceiling. Use incandescent lights if possible, since flourescent bulbs cause disturbances in the radios of the residents, distort color, and cause absence of shadow. The latter makes it difficult to judge distances in threading needles, cutting cloth, wood, etc.

Use of pull-down fixtures where close work is done, such as, at desk, work bench, or loom, will eliminate problems of vision for the elderly.

Electrical outlets should be located on all four walls at 10' intervals, and 40" from the floor.

One 220 volt outlet should be installed if a kiln for ceramics or enameling is planned.

9. *Equipment:*

Worktables: either oblong (8' x 3') or round (5' dia.) with pedestal type base. Work surface 29" - 31" from floor, so wheel chairs will slide under.

T.V. Tables: having 3 or 4 easily movable tables of this type for bedside, chairside, and loomside use is very handy.

Mobile Cart: which folds for efficient storage. These can be used as extra work space, for parties and bedside use, library, and carrying extra loads.

Arm Chairs: with cushions and straight backs.

Folding Chairs: 2 for emergency use.

Workbench: 36" high, with a low work section 30" high for men in wheelchairs.

Sink: With sludge trap, one basin 15" x 30" and 29" to 30" from the floor. This sink should be set into a counter with a minimum of 18" drainboard on each side, and cupboards or shelves underneath the counters. A single control mixer is good for one-handed people, and the sink should be left open underneath for wheelchairs. This sink can be in the bathroom or in the main work room.

Step-stool: for reaching high shelves.

Electric Vibrating Marker: for identification of equipment.

Adjustable Height Ironing Board and temperature control steam iron.
Sewing machines: one treadle and one electric portable with reverser and zigzag.
Desk, Telephone, File Cabinet & Typewriter: located in a secluded corner for use of the director.
Looms: for types and kinds, see Weaving Chapter, Sec. III., Chapter 22.
Adjustable height. over-the-bed table for use with wheelchairs which do not fit under the work table.
Game Storage Cupboard: for cards, Bingo, Scrabble, chess, dominoes, etc.

10. *Special Features (optional):*
    - 16 MM Projector and screen
    - Library shelves for books
    - Mimeograph equipment for newsletter, record forms, pattern copying, etc.
    - Tumbler for rock polishing
    - Ceramic and enameling kiln with 220 volt outlet
    - Camera for use in activities of senior citizens and employees
    - Floor loom
    - Display cabinet or shelves for completed work
    - Two folding card tables to set up for special projects when the regular work tables are in use.

11. *Materials:*
    The best advice we can give you in this area is—GO SLOWLY. Be sure you have a need and use for an item before you spend the money.
    The second bit of advice we offer is—BUY GOOD QUALITY.
    There are many books which list the necessary tools and materials for the various handicrafts. Use you local library for this help. If you wish to have your own copy of such lists, send for a copy of Evelyn Bengson's *A Guide To Planning & Equipping A Handicraft Facility For A Nursing Home Activity Program,* State Health Department, Olympia, Washington. Don't be afraid to ask help of craftsmen, arts and crafts teachers and use the Yellow Pages of your local telephone book as a resource aid.
    In addition, use the elderly and their knowledge, for they are the ones for whom you are acquiring the materials. They will love you for it and take a much more personal and active interest in the program if they have had a part in the original plans.

    This comparison list will be a good start for you:

WOMEN'S INTERESTS	*MEN'S INTERESTS*
Quiet and soft projects	Noisy and messy projects
Long-term projects	Short-term projects
(Women will carry over more	(Most men like to com-

easily than men. 1 to 2 weeks for a project)

Sewing projects—hand and machine

Weaving projects, large and small

Knitting and yarn projects

Personal interests in people

plete an item rather quickly. 1 to 2 days to complete)

Mosaic projects, large and small

Novelty use of weaving technique

Woodworking, usually small, short-term.

Scientific interests

From the comparisons you are able to start your own list of essential materials and supplies:

WOMEN	MEN
Patterns	Patterns
Cloth, yarn, thread, etc.	Wood, hammers, nails, etc.
Scissors, needles, thimbles	Tiles, grout, glue
	Saws, sandpaper
Knitting needles, crochet hooks	Vise, "C" clamps, etc.
Small weaving devices	

Lastly, the Activity Program Director will need some supplies and materials with which to operate the business end of the activity program.

Chapter 4

APPLYING THE
PROFESSIONAL APPROACH

> A helping hand
> Oft does more good
> Than either words
> Or money could.
>
> Alfred Tooke

The "helping hand" used in this bit of poetic philsophy is a very broad term for helping to supply the needs of people. Everyone has needs, old and young, sick and well. As an older person grows in years, he may suffer many kinds of losses. Some may be in real property, some in physical decline, and some in mental changes. He begins to feel left out, as though he is nobody and has no identity. His physical problems and disabilities may not be accepted by him or his family, and thus poor attitudes toward aging are developed. He is growing old, but this process started the day he was born and has been going on ever since.

Most of the elderly people you will encounter have not prepared themselves for what is happening to them, and are feeling depressed, frustrated, and discouraged. Perhaps they have multiple disabilites, slowed mental processes, may have had long periods of bedfastness and inactivity before coming to you. They are lonely and feel unwanted. Perhaps they feel insecure from loss of "a home" and from not being useful to themselves or to others. Sometimes their standards of cleanliness and sociability are at a low point.

You are presented with a depressed person and he is in your hands to return to whatever level of usefulness you both can achieve together.

PERSONAL NEEDS

The Latin term "primum, non nocere" means "first, do no harm." It is a good phrase to understand and put foremost in your mind. The whole person, not just the sick part of him, is your concern. Do nothing to harm this sensitive being. Consider his present physical and mental condition in an objective and highly individualized way. Try to keep an emotional equilibrium with him so that progress can be made. Try to help him accept the inevitable and not rebel against it; for with the rebellion of the spirit no progress can be made. His needs in terms of progress are many. They will be fulfilled by those who now surround him, provide for his physical needs and for the stimulation of his mental and emotional growth.

1. First the elderly person needs good care and medical treatment to reach the highest physical and mental ability possible, and to maintain it once it is reached. This health program involves the doctor, the registered nurse, the licensed practical nurse, the nurse's aide, the registered physical therapist, the registered occupational therapist, the dietitian, perhaps speech and respiration therapists, to say nothing of the housekeepers and maintenance staff, over a long period of time, all working together with this common goal in mind.

2. Love and warm affection, sincerely given by all those involved in the senior citizen's health program, are almost as important as his pills—and sometimes more so! If you do not like body contact, hugging and hand-holding, geriatrics is not for you. Unlimited tender loving care is the rule here. Be sure to know his name and use it frequently.

3. Third, security is needed as provided by dependable people. A clean room and bed, prompt answers to requests, regular and adequate meals, carrying out your promises, all give the patient a feeling of relaxed comfort and individuality. In this atmosphere he starts feeling better and seeing progress, and so develops a more secure attitude to go forward faster. Be sure he has something of his own from the start, a Bible, a small plant, a clock, or a stuffed toy for company. Take good care of his personal possessions and clothing if he is unable to do so for himself.

4. Recognition and status as an individual within the group is the fourth necessity. Stop to talk about something of mutual interest—the weather, a construction project in the street or building, a news headline, or merely a current joke. Keep a light-hearted attitude and give him a chance to have his say. Use a great amount of tact. This is essential for the senior citizen to have a feeling of importance and a place in the group.

5. Everyone needs new experiences in fellowship. Making new friends

within a group takes some doing for some people. Perhaps you can help by picking out another person in the group who has a similar attitude. As they become acquainted they can help one another, not only in physical aspects but psychologically also. The buddy system works all through life. Encourage them to take part in the spiritual life of the group, reading, visiting with ministers, attending church services. The social involvement will soon create a feeling of being "in," being wanted, and being a part of something interesting.

6. People need respect and understanding from those around them. Give each one a chance to express his ideas and use them when you can. His personal dignity is very important and must be encouraged. Do not belittle him in any way, even if his behavior is baffling at times. Remember that he has "plus" qualities gained from long years of living. His knowledge in some area will benefit you if you are receptive and perceptive. Develop a keen sense of what to do and say in order to maintain good relations with him and avoid offense. It will never hurt you to give compliments and make pleasant, happy comments. His confidence in you will grow and grow!

7. Provide an atmosphere for creative expression to occupy his time and abilities. The fulfillment of this need should result in a satisfying sense of achievement for the elderly person. His enjoyment of hobbies earlier in life make it easier now. If there have been no interests other than vocation you may find it difficult to arouse an interest and exercise it. Carefully choose an activity based on the needs of a family member, friend, or perhaps even the vocation. Older people are practical. You will have to give him a reason for your choice of project. It should be geared to:

   a. the physical, mental, and emotional abilities of the person.
   b. an area of interest and familiarity to him.
   c. give a sense of encouragement to him.
   d. a resulting product of which he can be proud.

Minimize his errors and maximize his genuine successes. He may want to stop working before he should. Encourage him to continue a little longer, to a point of fulfillment, but not resulting in over-fatigue. The old saying, "The best angle from which to approach anything is the *try* angle," certainly comes in handy here. You may have to try several times, and end up with a good friendship and no material progress. But having that friend has been just what the person needed. Keep your sights on a balance of work, play, love, and worship.

8. Encourage your new friend to make decisions toward future goals and independence. First of all, try to have him learn to express himself in a controlled and socially acceptable manner. This will lead to the initiation of ideas on his part. Soon he will be able to set some goals for himself. All of these do not have to be outwardly visible. They may be

goals for physical progress; improvement of his memory (by use of
repetitive tasks); deepening of his concentration abilities (by use of
projects requiring full attention); or perhaps greater relaxation, acceptance, and improved ease in living.

The atmosphere and attitude in which these needs are met are
the ingredients which count toward a good response from patients in
any kind of institution or group setting. The attitude of the staff,
and the tone of the atmosphere in which activities are conducted, are
much more important to the older person's well-being, adjustment,
and progress, than are the activities themselves. If he finds himself in
an unhappy and discouraging environment, chances are that he will
never participate in any way. So, everyone connected with senior
citizens must contribute toward the encouraging climate necessary
for each to be at his best.

A professional approach, yet not an unconcerned one, must be
used by each staff member. Workers, without some training and
understanding of elderly people, tend to become involved in the
older person's problems, life and illnesses, resulting in a loss of effec-
tiveness in their duties. It is important for you to put your heart and
soul into your work, sincerely and honestly, while on duty—but
free your mind when you leave the building.

YOUR APPROACH—BE DIFFERENT

In working with people, there is no place for mediocrity, particularly with older people. The root of the word "mediocre" means
middle or ordinary. It also has a connotation of below average, of
poor quality and sub-standard. If mediocrity is used in dealing with
older people, who already have personality stresses and physical pain,
it cannot create the warm, comfortable feeling necessary for the
organization, the elderly, their families, and all the personnel
involved in the activities.

Many influences today tend to level all of us into being a mediocre people, all of whom do the same things in the same way—afraid
to be different. But, to be different, with a new and unusual
approach, is needed. The following are a couple of ideas that have
worked for us:

1. Make little felt mice on hair clips. (Pattern in Section III, Chapter 15)
   Use them as "cheerer-uppers" and conversation pieces by clipping
   them on the collar or pocket of a senior citizen, family or staff member, with the instruction to pass it on to anyone who needs the lift and
   cheer brought by the little mouse.
2. Make a wall chart, which we call a mood indicator sign. (Figure 4-1)

TODAY I AM

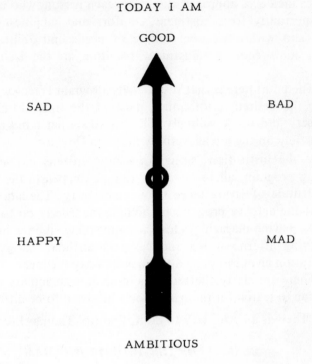

Figure 4-1

The arrow revolves on a paper fastener and has a feather opposite the point. Use gay colors, and assign it to someone who needs a lift or who has been reluctant to participate. The idea is, of course, that the recipient of the sign indicates to you his or her mood and you react accordingly. It is surprising how a small thing like this will change moods and raise spirits.

3. If you really want to win their cooperation, to say nothing of their admiration and respect for you, learn to converse with the senior citizens in their native tongue—Spanish, Swedish, or a little of a native Indian jargon. A little goes a long way when greeting them each morning.

Each person must be regarded as an individual with physical, mental, and social problems peculiar to him, particularly if he is in an institution where there are many of his station living together. His needs must be met by the entire staff on this basis.

In the activity program, there may be as many different projects as there are patients at work. Those who wish to stay in their rooms also should be offered appropriate activities which can be directed with less personal attention from the Activity Program Director. This is not a mediocre approach and offers each person, who is interested, an opportunity for adjustment, comfort, and happiness on his own terms and within his own sphere of needs and abilities. A good feeling and successful adjustment, resulting, are the desired end products.

The point here is that the Activity Program Director, in order to secure the desired result, must, most of the time, do more than is necessary and do it willingly. She has to set her mind and energies completely on the job as Activity Program Director.

If the institution caring for senior citizens has an in-service training program, all of the staff can be steeped in the philosophy and attitude of giving more than is necessary. The aides become a part of the activity program by helping the elderly get to their destinations, having magazines close at hand, tying ribbons in their hair, or serving afternoon tea and cake on birthday party days. This cooperation gives everyone a warm and happy feeling.

There are always better ways to operate an activity program, so continue to search for them and don't be afraid to be different.

"There is a better way to do it, find it." Thomas Edison.

BENEFITS OF THE ACTIVITY PROGRAM

1. *To the Senior Citizen:*
    Use of time and abilities
    Encouragement to maintain health level
    Socialization and fellowship
    Acceptance as a member of a group
    Personal recognition
    Sense of accomplishment
    Development of goal setting
    New contacts with outsiders
2. *To the Staff:*
    Helps make personal care more attractive
    Makes working with the aged easier
    Broadens concept of personal care
    Helps in understanding the individual
    Pinpoints awareness to individual needs and potential
    Integrates staff into program
3. *To the Public*
    Understanding of the aims of the institution
    Awareness of responsibility toward others
    Participation through volunteer efforts and material contribution
    Acceptance as part of the health and medical care program

There is an old story told of how it was once the custom in the ancient country of Asia Minor to take the older folks to a cave, away from the immediate family surroundings, so that the remainder of their lives could be lived out in the peace and quiet their nature craved. Of course, this put them out of people's way.

Preparations were being made to take an aged grandfather to the Cave of the Old Ones, from which none returned. A young son, obedient to his father's request, brought a woolen blanket for his grandfather, but he neglected to say that he had cut it in two, leaving the second half at home. Upon returning from the cave, where the grandfather had been disposed of with proper filial respect, the father discovered the other half of the blanket. He scolded the son for being so stingy, because he had cut the blanket in two. "No Father," the lad replied, "I wasn't being stingy. I thought it was better to give Grandpa only half, then later I could give the other half to you." Needless to say this shocked the father. Upon recovering, the father said to the son, "Come, let's go back to the cave and bring Grandfather home."

The moral of this story is evident; the idea of putting yourself in other people's shoes is a very humane and kindly attitude, and one we should all adopt.

Bibliography

Bengson, Evelyn M., Guide to Planning and Equipping Handi-craft Facility for a Nursing Home Activity Program. State Department of Health, Olympia, Washington. 1964.

Committee on Aging, A New Concept of Aging, American Medical Association, 535 North Dearborn St., Chicago, Illinois, 60610.

Council on Medical Service. How the Older Person Can Get the Most out of Living, American Medical Association, 535 North Dearborn St., Chicago, Illinois, 60610.

Hildenbrand, Grace C., Found Horizons for the Aging. New York City Home for Dependents, Welfare Island, N.Y., N.Y., 1948.

Chapter 5

MOTIVATING THE ELDERLY
FOR DESIRED RESULTS

The purpose of an activity program is to stimulate people to do things, to stir up interest and desire which lead to mental and physical motion. Just providing things to do isn't enough; people must somehow be drawn out of themselves and into an activity which will provide the pleasure and satisfaction of accomplishment.

As a general rule there are three kinds of humans in the world: the very few who make things happen, the slightly larger number who take part in what is happening, and the overwhelming majority who have no idea what is happening. This division exists every bit as much in a health care facility as anywhere else. The great majority of the patients won't even know that an activity program exists, let alone voluntarily take part in it. You have to influence these people; you have to get them to want to take part. You have to motivate them.

What is motivation? Our definition is simple. Motivation is that which you do to cause someone else to do what you want him to do. Or, in reverse order, to get a person to *do* something, you must cause him to *want to* do it, and *that which you do* to bring this about is your method of motivation.

That which is many things, big and little, mostly little. It is nearly as many things as there are people, because that which you do is different for each person, and it may well be different again for the same person at another time. Encouraging people—especially sick and elderly people—to do what you want them to do is not at all simple. The only simple thing about it is that you must have love in your heart and sincere concern in your mind. You can't fudge about this; either the love and concern are there or they are not. If you are prepared to offer the necessary affection and attention, you can always find a *that which* to motivate interest and action for a particular situation.

MAKE THE FIRST CONTACTS COUNT

Because a new patient is usually too confused, frightened or ill to originate friendly contact with anyone, it is up to you to start things off right. Always smile, even before words are spoken, even if silence lasts for days or weeks. Give a hug or hand squeeze to the affectionate patient who needs it. When conversation does begin, listen. If listening means long pauses, leave long pauses. Maybe your patient just wants to rest, maybe he wants a chance to think up his own kind of contribution to the discussion, or maybe he wants to change the subject, in which case you will find out what interests him and what his *want to* area is. The first contacts with each patient are important confidence-builders, make them count by showing affection, interest and sincere admiration for whatever is admirable about him.

RESPECT PERSONAL DIGNITY

Each patient's room is his home while he is with you, so knock on the door before entering his "house." Announce yourself with a word of greeting or wave of the hand; move slowly (the patient wants to watch what you do in his private area); do not intrude on personal privacy by forcing anyone to talk with you before he is ready.

INSPIRE RESPECT

Mediocrity won't motivate much. To build the confidence which makes people want to do things with and for you, you must exemplify the best in patient relations. Three particularly good ways to be outstanding are:

- Do what you say you will do, always and with confidence.
- Share attention among your patients as equally as possible; when with each one give your undivided effort and skill to him alone.
- Create respect by honest thoughtfulness. Bring each person some little thing, something he can keep, such as, a pencil or pad of paper, a thimble, a flower, or a pretty leaf.

KNOW YOUR PATIENTS

A friend of ours who lives in the country keeps his lawn free of mole hills by placing traps in the particular spot each mole will visit next. He has phenomenal success at catching the little pests because he has learned to think like a mole; he has enough knowledge of their habits to know just what each one will do next. The same principle applies to controlling people; you have to know their likes, dislikes, personal habits and whatever else affects the direction they will take. Pay special attention to sensitive areas (relatives, religion, money, national origin, etc.) which might create emotional static. Remember what each person tells you about himself, and, even though you learn things about him elsewhere, refer only to what he has told you when you are with him. Try to think as the patient thinks. Learn his line of logic, however peculiar it may be, so that you can predict what he will do next.

MAKE HASTE SLOWLY

Only the muscular or the foolhardy will attempt to change the direction of a large moving object or a determined human being by direct confrontation. A wise person will go along with the situation for a while, then will gradually change the direction of motion after getting a feel for the conditions. Because natural human resistance to new things is magnified by age and illness, you must begin with little things, watching for the slightest interest from your subject, and taking advantage of every opportunity to utilize that interest—not suddenly or obviously but with a steady push. Progress comes by inches; be sure that each inch is in the direction you want to go.

MATCH ACTIVITY TO INDIVIDUAL NEED

People are like hotel rooms; each has a different key, a different way to get past reserve and apprehension to open the door of interest. Because activities are the keys, each one you select must fit a patient and his needs. The following are some examples of keyed activities:

- Clothing repair and button replacement—for a woman who is concerned about her appearance.
- A new game of solitaire (there are dozens of them)—to create a feeling of individual proficiency.

- Flower arrangement—may lead the patient outdoors and perhaps eventually to active garden work.
- Language instruction from a foreign-speaking patient—puts the instructor, at least, on firm ground and each word or phrase learned brings you closer to him.
- A small personal service by you—wrap a gift, write a letter, wash a sweater. Something which involves the person, even though he only sits and watches, is an activity which will lead eventually to more involvement.
- A trip to the activity room, just to watch—the watching will often turn into active interest in what the busy people there are doing.

But remember: pleasure and satisfaction must result from whatever activity you get the patient into, or both of you will wind up in an unhappy grind. You may be willing to put up with this condition, but the patient won't.

MATCH ACTIVITY TO PHYSICAL AND MENTAL CONDITION

Knowledge of each patient's limitations is essential—you can lose an entire campaign in a few minutes if you stimulate desire for a goal which is physically or mentally unattainable. Some limitations to watch out for are:

- Eyesight—hands stiff? arm action restricted?
- Mental ability—alert and inquisitive? sluggish?
- Attention span—long, short, or non-existent?
- Scope of interest—entirely self-centered? or can a new idea get in?

When you discover what the limitations are in each case you will know the kinds of activities into which the patient can safely be motivated. That doesn't mean that you will ever get him there, but at least you know what to attempt. The worse the physical or mental condition, the slower the progress; be ready to move slowly. Give the patient time to think about and react to your ideas; the more limitations, the more time.

UNDERSTAND SENIOR CITIZENS LIKES AND NEEDS

Likes:

- Familiar things
- Things involving children
- Talking about old things (like making ice cream by hand)
- Singing hymns and old-time songs

- Listening to others sing hymns and old-time songs
- Doing things they used to do (making cookies, carding wool)
- Quiet periods and naps
- Food (but be careful about special diets)
- Complaining

Needs:

- Understanding, love and affection
- Warm cozy sweaters
- Lap robes
- Pillows
- Time to themselves
- Happy smiling people around them
- Things going on, which they can take or leave

Use these wants and needs to help bring about the essential conditions of attention, interest, confidence and friendship to motivate people to do what you want them to do. Progress will vary from day to day, and you will not always be making the headway you would like, but conceal your concern and be encouraging. Be encouraging even when you must devise four or five different ways to explain some simple operation, and when you have to avoid blaming anyone for the failures. ("Well now, that didn't quite work out did it? This must be one of those days. Now let's try it this way.")

"The most important motive for work in the school and in life," said Albert Einstein, "is the pleasure in work, pleasure in its result, and the knowledge of the value of the result to the community." The little 92-year-old lady pumping the treadle of an empty sewing machine and chatting happily to herself about the days gone by may not seem to be creating much of value, but her pleasure is just as much a product of your activity program as are the wooden toy trains and stuffed animals created by people who are capable of a much higher level of accomplishment.

You and your patients will find pleasure in work, in its result, and in its value to the community when *that which* you do motivates the people under your care to *want to do* the things which give them the most individual satisfaction.

Chapter 6

WORKING SUCCESSFULLY
WITH GROUPS

Working effectively with groups of people in a happy, friendly, constructive manner, takes some doing, some planning, and a good deal of nimbleness of wit. Not all people like to work or play in groups. It will not be hard to discover this. Upon observation, notice if a senior citizen sits and walks apart from others, does not verbalize readily as he passes another, and seems like a loner. Beware of pushing him into a group. It may not work.

If he chooses just one friend, or two, and restricts himself to talking only with them, he may be hard to include in a group.

If the person is demonstrative, he will let you know positively and definitely that he wants to work alone, or in his room. Or, perhaps he just wants to be left alone.

If he is timid, you may learn it through physical and emotional symptoms, such as, tears, expression of fears, or inability to cope with the normal confusion which usually accompanies a group of people working or playing closely together. This is something an Activity Program Director learns by experience. After it happens once, you won't forget it soon. The result usually disrupts the whole group until their attention can be distracted into some constructive channel.

Not long ago, acting upon the orders of an elderly person's physician, an Activity Program Director brought a recent hemiplegic, who was in a depressed state, to a full workshop of people. The idea was to cheer her, give her new ideas, and thus a new outlook toward her future. It was hoped that this would help the therapists' work with her psychologically while they strengthened her physical limitations. Shortly after being introduced to the group, some of whom were severely handicapped, she began to tremble more and more obviously, until she finally collapsed in tears, with her head on the table. The Activity Program Director removed her unobtrusively from the room, and the episode was reported to the nurse. Upon investigation it was learned that the woman had never liked groups, and could not, even when she was well, cope with many things going on around her all at one time. She had lived a hermit-like life, with her own home and yard, and few neighbors and relatives. A group atmosphere was normally repulsive to her, and especially more so when she was ill.

This story leads to the first principle in working with groups of people.

1. *Be sure you are familiar with the people and the projects on which they will be working.* Spend some time just talking with each person to learn his interests before you make suggestions. In this way you can assure yourself of his physical, mental, and emotional abilities for work. You will be able to determine whether he is a loner or able to work in a group. It is not always advisable for an older person to be required to interact with others. Sometimes it is beneficial and sometimes not. Interest can be aroused by carrying with you a couple of samples of finished projects, not too complicated but attractive.

2. *Try to limit the number of different projects being done in the same area.* As an example, if a man is grouting a mosaic piece, hand washing is necessary before the Activity Program Director can go to help the lady at the loom or to thread a needle. Involve as many people in the production of one type of article as possible over a long period, as long as it is mutually interesting. However, take care not to have all of the people doing the same thing at the same time. This can produce over-competition and friction. ("Why don't you do it my way?" "My system is better." "I'm just wasting my time doing what everyone else does.") Elderly people are notorious for wanting to do things in their way and with their own system. Many times it is a better way. They like to show and tell how much they have learned from living as long as they have.

3. *Break projects down into small, simple parts.* Everyone can contribute a different process toward a community project. In this way each person can take credit for having helped. The end result will be complicated but the individual parts for each person will have been simple. Perhaps the project which will attract the interest of a

resident is part of a larger one, possibly a single crocheted square for an afghan. Several people can work on this activity. The written instructions to each person are identical, but you will coach each person in accordance with his needs, capabilities, and speed of comprehension. To have had a part in the construction of this larger, end result will provide recognition, pride, and self-esteem to each person in the group.

4. *Don't assign extensive projects.* Elderly people need to have short processes, one color of yarn, one piece of pattern at a time to understand. At age 80-90 it is·unusual to find someone who can take a four piece pattern, whether to be constructed of wood or cloth, and follow it through to completion. One step at a time is the rule.

   Don't confuse him with too much information, too many instructions, or an overabundance of materials all at once. Give instructions in his area of comprehension and in his mental, emotional, and manual abilities. Don't even let him see what comes next until his mind has progressed to that point. Then be ready to produce the next step. If he expresses concern for the ultimate outcome, assure him you know how to do it and you will guide him to completion. You may have to do this repeatedly, but each time make it sound as if it is the first time.

5. *Don't expect fast results or rapid progress.* You may get it, but this is the exception rather than the rule. One exception is a wiry little lady who worked as a power machine seamstress in the New York City clothing industry. She wants a project to do all by machine—no hand work. She works quickly for she remembers her pay was on piece work production, and her mind still goes at that speed. Once in awhile you will run across this type of prolific producer, and it takes much planning to keep them busy while still satisfying the slower producer and evening out the attention to each individual.

6. *Be sure the article is useful to the senior citizen, his family, or friends.* Perhaps you can dispose of it to benefit the program. It should at least be designed to have a purpose when completed. It will be more attractive and useful if good color, design principles, proportions, and material combinations are used in its planning and development. Even plastic bleach bottle articles can be most useful and desirable if good art principles are used in their construction.

7. *Arrange the physical set-up of the work room in an orderly and workable fashion.* This is important to the general operation. Be able to open cupboard doors without moving furniture, tables, and chairs. Place work areas so there are few distractions nearby. This will encourage concentration. Keep supplies and materials available and within easy reach. Men and women need to work together in the same general area. Don't separate them. The personal habits of each

will be improved and they will take an interest in each other's work and progress. A personal concern and helpful attitude will result. This is beneficial to a good activity program.

8. *Place ambulatory people in harder to reach locations and reserve accessible areas for wheelchairs.* Transfer the patients from wheelchairs to the workroom arm chairs. Fold and store the wheelchairs. This will create more room in the work area. Place the same type of workers together and have them face each other if possible. This will encourage conversation, and many times reassurance and help. Those who need constant supervisiion can be seated in the easiest location for the Activity Director to reach. The more capable ones can sit farther away. A lazy susan in the middle of the table with basic needs for the activity at hand will save steps. Think ahead and place the needed items there before the workers come.

9. *Wear clothing which helps you in your work.* A shirt or smock with large pockets for necessities, pencil, paper, small bandage scissors, keys, etc., will save many steps. Duplicate sets of some items located throughout the work area will be helpful to all.

10. *Always try to be patient.* Keep your wits. Never become ruffled. If you are needed to help in several places at once, keep calm and don't let anyone know you might be disturbed. Start a conversation, something for them to think about while you undo and fix. If by some accident your feelings do get the better of you, and you show some loss of composure, turn it into a humorous situation. Make a joke of everything you can, especially if it is on you. The older people will laugh and think more of you for it. Instead of saying, "Just a minute," say, "Put down your work and relax awhile, then I'll be there." Call their attention to something out of the window to divert their eyes. Refer to something you have put on the bulletin board or the location of the barometer needle that morning. Avoid controversial subjects which might whet tempers with verbal disagreements. Try using a universal joke, one which everyone would think humorous.

> *For example:* "My husband and his friend went fishing from a boat on Pine Lake (use a local lake) last Saturday. They hit a good spot and caught their limit in ten minutes. They want to return to this spot, so they marked an X on the boat!" It may take a couple of minutes, but they'll get it.

11. *If things get out of step, and nothing is meshing, try a change of pace.* This will happen in the best planned activity program, so call a halt to what is being done and have a tea party or a coffee klatch. Turn on a little battery-operated tooting train and let it walk among their feet. Any similar attention-getting device will work. A change of interest is good for everyone.

12. *Some elderly people can take the correction or redoing of their work in front of a group; others would be discouraged.* Experience in working with people will tell you which is which. In general, the person who has a positive outlook, uses definite word usage, and actions, who likes you, can stand to have his work corrected. The person who is of a weaker, more timid personality, who may sigh or lean back in his chair tired and exhausted—this is the person to handle gently. If a piece of work absolutely has to be repaired or corrected by you, do it when you are alone. And if the owner of the work notices it, which he may not, say, "Oh, didn't I do it right?" or something which puts the blame on you. Let the older person tell you something about it if he cares to do so.

13. *Always have an encouraging attitude with senior citizens.* Find something good to say to them, about themselves, their work, their ideas, and their ways. Everyone has good points; it's your job to find them.

14. *Use a great amount of tact in handling a group of elderly people.* Remember they have lived, in most cases, longer than you have. Their knowledge in some area will benefit you if you are receptive and perceptive. Tact is essential because it makes the older person feel important and have a place in the group. Develop this keen sense of what to do and say in order to maintain good relations with others and avoid offense. It will never hurt you to give compliments and make pleasant, happy comments. It will make their confidence in you grow. Don't permit yourself to show temper. When you are right, you can afford to keep your temper;—when you are wrong, you can't afford to lose it!

GROUP ACTIVITIES

Resident Council: Weekly meetings.

For guidelines to types of activities.

To organize activities.

To implement activities.

(Where capable people are available, this can be a very helpful group.)

Food Conference: Weekly meetings with dietician and cook.

For exchange of suggestions and ideas.

To allow residents to have something to do with food choices and combinations.

Exercise Classes: Daily with a physical education or physical therapist leader.

Very stimulating activity.

Exercises done in sitting position.

Ambulatory residents can help non-ambulatory in coming and going to classes.

	Creates regular and definite time of day to exercise.
	(You'll need a large room, after about two weeks, for word will spread fast.)
Discussion Groups:	Bring a good leader from outside of facility.
	This takes time to get started and become acquainted with leader. Be sure the leader knows of interest and development lag.
	After a few weeks, this becomes a must with the alert residents.
Regular Religious Services:	At least weekly.
	Facilities operated by religious groups will have daily services.
	Contact local or regional ministerial association so an alternating of faiths can be arranged. Then, every resident will have opportunity to enjoy his choice.
	Large print hymn book is helpful.
Afternoon Tea:	Schedule at regular time daily.
	Kitchen cart with coffee, tea, juice, and crackers.
	Centrally located.
	Gives the elderly a social time to which they will look forward.
Recreation Groups:	Films, games, and music.
	Regular time and place.
	Provides an opportunity for them to be somewhere and do something.

In most large cities, there is a Council on Aging, Community Center for the Aging, or similar organization which is usually a member of the United Good Neighbors or Community Fund Organization. It will coordinate all community groups and activity groups for the senior citizen and retired individual. Contacting them can supply many new ideas, both for inside and outside your facility. Ask to be added to their mailing list.

SCHEDULING:

The question of scheduling becomes an individual problem to be solved by the Administrator, the Activity Program Director, and the needs and desires of the senior citizens of the facility. There are, however, some basics around which the schedule should be arranged.

The participants have more energy and are more interested in doing things during the morning and early part of the afternoon. By late afternoon and evening they want to sit, watch, and be entertained. With the cooperation of departments regular activities such as exercise class, church, etc., can be held in the mornings.

Visiting of relatives, friends, and trips for the elderly, all interrupt the regular routine. Also the treatment programs of the nursing, physical therapy, and occupational therapy departments have to be met on a regular basis to work all of them into the resident's day. So, a flexible routine in the activity room seems to be best.

At Issaquah Villa the activity room door is never closed. Projects and equipment are always available to those interested. This arrangement is made for the convenience of the resident, not for the Activity Program Director. It is a hard schedule for her, with no set pattern or hourly time for individuals to come and go. Gradually she will be able to arrange a satisfactory routine, still being flexible. If she manages to be available in the workroom at a certain time each day, the residents will soon become accustomed to this and come when she is there. Some senior citizens will prefer to work in their rooms and these can be seen later in the day to check progress and need for help.

Due to the many factors stated above, the regular work crew will vary in numbers from day to day. Sometimes the room will be overflowing, and at other times one will wonder where all the workers are.

If the Activity Program Director is a part-time employee, then the desires of the Administrator and the needs of the residents should determine the hours and schedule. If it is felt that group activities such as bingo, games, parties, films, discussions, etc., are needed most, then the schedule should be arranged accordingly. If a craft program is desired, additional arrangements should be made.

Grouping of specific types of elderly people together in a work session might be considered as part of the scheduling arrangement. For example, have the confused and disoriented group at one time, the mentally alert at another.

A good Activity Program Director will plan some form of activity on weekends with the help of volunteers. This could be music for Sunday afternoons, or a church group with slides or films on Sunday evenings. Dancing recitals, gay music, and young people to entertain and visit can be scheduled for Saturday afternoons and evenings. A variety of activities is the ultimate goal, to try to please each resident at some time.

Here is a suggested schedule for weekdays:

9:00 a.m.-12:00 noon—Individuals and groups in work room

12:00-1:00 p.m.—Lunch & help with individual requests

1:00 p.m.-2:00 p.m.—Individuals and groups in work room

2:00 p.m.—4:00 p.m.—Group activities, games, recreation, entertainment, tea

4:00 p.m.-5:00 p.m.—See individuals in rooms, clean-up, and preparation time for Activity Program Director

Evenings—Visitors, films, slides

Planning with much flexibility makes a good schedule.

Chapter 7

WINNING THE
COOPERATION OF
VOLUNTEERS AND
OUTSIDE HELP

A volunteer is "one who offers himself of his own free will for a service, without valuable consideration or any legal obligation." This definition, from Webster's Dictionary, is accurate, as far as it goes. This chapter will define, offer suggestions, and make additional observations about volunteers.

Those who are grouped under the general classification of volunteers come in all ages, with all manner of skills which will supplement and add to those of the regular staff. They present new faces and refreshing approaches in activities.

Good volunteers have to be sought out. Some craftsmen, or persons with a special talent or knowledge, will offer their time readily to activity programs. These volunteers who come of their own will are usually people with drive and motivation, and, if guided in the right direction, can be of much help to the Activity Program Director. They will tell you what they like and are able to do, and make suggestions. Sometimes you have to pry it out of them, but this is where the Activity Program Director shapes and guides the program for the benefit of all.

Remember, they have no incentive in the form of remuneration, so try to give them some kind of satisfaction in pleasure and good experiences. Put yourself in their shoes.

It is difficult to keep volunteers helping and not hindering your program. They can occupy all of your time if you are not careful. Give each one a definite, independent job; sometimes in pairs, depending upon their personality, ability, skill, and interest. Two volunteers at a time are all one director can incorporate into the program, unless she has had a great deal of experience. Your space, facilities, volume of patients to be served, and program organization, will all affect the number of volunteers to be utilized at one time.

Volunteers do not represent authority to the individual resident, and should be given your support. They do represent the needed contact with the outside community if the senior citizen is confined to an institution or his own home.

HOW TO GET VOLUNTEERS

Recruitment of volunteers is a very personal thing. Decide first whether they are to be used in your facility, and who will direct them once they are there. This is an administrative decision and is covered in this chapter's section on "How to Use Volunteers."

The person who will direct their functions should do the recruiting and securing of volunteers. If she has been selected for the job she already has an "in" among her friends, her community, her organizations and club life. She should be familiar with the areas in her program which can use volunteer help.

If the Volunteer Director does not live in the general area of the facility location, she should *spend time and careful effort becoming acquainted with what happens, who makes it happen, and why it happens the way it does,* in the area surrounding the facility location. She should look into available services and resources. Here we mean people services, but while she is doing this, she is making herself and her needs known, and material resources will develop. File this information away for future use. *What churches, clubs, community groups, and service organizations are available?* What organized park, recreation, Y.M.C.A., school, library, etc., groups are there? Meet the people who are the leaders and arrange to go to their regular meetings to become acquainted with them. Visit the tradespeople, and do your shopping for the facility as locally as possible so they will feel they are a part of your program.

What health facilities are available; i.e., visiting nurse, nursing homes, hospital, medical clinics? You may want to become a member of a local Business & Professional Women's Club, or

Women's Club, to have a more personal contact with the nearby sources of volunteers and materials. If a man is doing the recruiting, it may be fruitful for him to join a Kiwanis, Rotary, or Elks Club.

Public relations enter into this recruitment, and follow it through to the development of volunteers. The local newspaper will be able to supply club and organization contacts. Also, the Chamber of Commerce has monthly meetings which can prove very enlightening about attitudes toward the elderly in the community.

Volunteers come from any group, any age, and any kind of home. The recruiter will have to spend time out making calls to get results.

The following is a list of clubs and service groups to contact for volunteers:

Garden Clubs	Friends of the Library
4-H Clubs	Eastern Star
Campfire & Horizon	DeMolay
Girl Scouts	Rainbow
Boy Scouts	Chamber of Commerce
Kiwanis	Junior Chamber of Commerce
Rotary	Junior Chamber Wives
Lions & Auxiliary	Church Guilds & Circles
Eagles & Auxiliary	Golden Age Clubs
Business & Professional Women	Tape Clubs
Toastmaster & Toastmistress Clubs	Grandmother's Clubs
League of Women Voters	Sororities
Saddle, Pony, & Horse Clubs	Alumni Groups
County Agricultural Homemakers Clubs	
Small personal interest groups	
(Cards, knitting, book reviews, etc.)	

If your contact with each group provided one interested person, you would have a large group of volunteers to utilize. Most groups will ask what they, as a group, can do to help you. Have answers ready. Give them lists of waste materials they can save for you. Make suggestions concerning services which will not involve them in additional meetings. Offer to provide them with patterns and materials for project preparation for your program, such as, stuffed toys, animals, and dolls. Ask them to remember each birthday with a card or a fresh flower. They can save nylon hose for stuffing, or knick-knacks for bingo prizes. Indicate that you will be happy to pick up these donations. They might like to adopt an elderly person who has no family. This works wonderfully well with young peoples' groups. Individual teenagers may like to have an older person to visit and help. Tray favors, place mats, and party cookies are always welcome when donated. The young mothers in many of these groups will welcome the opportunity to help others, while staying home with the children. They can bake diabetic cookies for parties, or cut out and sew up toys to be stuffed.

The Golden Age Group will be happy to make lap robes for less ambulatory people if you'll supply the material. The local upholstery shop has numerous scraps and samples of cloth and drapery fabrics. Ask the local Tape Club to bring their next interesting tape exchange for your visually handicapped people to hear. Better still, ask volunteers to pick up four or five people and take them to the Tape Club meeting. Gradually you may work individuals out of the group who have the time and interest to become a successful individual volunteer.

There are also young people from Campfire, Scouts, etc., who are required to give community service for their credits. If the Activity Program Director will speak to these groups, a nucleus of capable "Volunteens" will develop.

Anytime a patient's family member or a good friend says, "Call me anytime I can help," make a note of her name and phone number in your 3" x 5" card reference file for the next time some shopping needs to be done. One word of caution concerning a resident's family member becoming a regular volunteer inside the facility; care must be taken that the personal involvement does not affect attitude and quality of work.

Someone who loves to play the piano and sing may offer to help with the musical activities, and you gain a music chairman for your volunteers. Let her get acquainted with a few of the senior citizens and pretty soon what they want, and what she has to offer by way of musical friends, will result in a regular schedule of music.

Junior Women's Clubs, whose members are now raising families, but who need the service credits and want to keep their hands in business techniques, will double up on baby sitting, thus allowing members to come once a week. They can cut stencils, run the mimeo, produce the monthly newsletter, do mending, call bingo, address bulk mail, and deliver and return films from the public library.

If you are fortunate in being located near a convent or other religious residence, there's sure to be someone living there who will come on a regular schedule to do things, such as, show films, read to the aged, or lead discussion groups.

When you get behind on dressing your looms, find a local hand weaver who will be happy to have you bring looms, one at a time, to be warped. She might even have odds and ends of materials to use in doing it.

Fit the job to the volunteer carefully. If you keep your mind working, soon you'll begin to see results from your efforts Keep forging ahead with ideas and contacts. Some Mondays you will be greeted by boxes and bags of goodies to use and notes of, "Call me when I can help!"

There have been many books written to help in using volunteers. They have descriptions of forms, lists, organization charts, etc.

For the use of the average Activity Program Director whose day is already very full without numerous charts and forms, we would like to list the mechanics of our operation.

I. *Initial Contact.* (See section in this chapter on "How to Get Volunteers.") By telephone, as a result of talking to a group, or a request for fulfillment of community service credits. Make appointment for personal interview.

II. *Personal Interview,* at the Activity Program Director's convenience, the applicant fills in the Interest Questionnaire. It is designed to be used for all ages. We review the form with the applicant, questioning as we go for additional background, such as: which religious group (organization memberships), what talent (amateur magician, yoga student, Bonsai maker, champ bowler, or flower arranger). You will find different information listed under the three sections—Hobbies, Interests, and Talents. Therefore, we leave in all three. We do not add long lists of crafts here to be checked, because we feel this limits their viewpoint as to how they would be utilized into the program. We would rather ask for specific areas of ability.

ISSAQUAH VILLA CONVALESCENT
OCCUPATIONAL THERAPY DEPT.

Interest Questionnaire

Name_____Telephone No. _____

Address_____ Zip_____

Days available _____ Weekly _____Monthly_____

Hours available   A.M. _____   P.M.   Evenings: On call: _____

Married _____Single _____ Children (ages) _____

Do you like old people _____Sick old people _____

Schooling completed (grade) _____

Student now_____ Where_____

Area of study _____

Special training _____

Occupation _____

Hobbies: Interests:

Scouts, Campfire, etc.: Are you a Member_____Are you a leader_____

Do you have a special talent: Please list:

Organization Memberships:

Comments to make your work here more effective:

_____

Under comments for more effective work, we list the motivating feature which brought them in the beginning. Sometimes you have to pry this out with several questions, but it will aid you in providing proper guidance for helping them to become better volunteers. A tour of the facility and introduction to key staff is included.

III. Fill in a 3" x 5" personal reference card, to be filed under "Volunteers" in the resource file and easily used by the Activity Program Director when the need arises.

_____

Name_____Telephone_____

Address_____Zip_____
Abilities (list briefly)

_____

(Leave blank for notes or dates of service you might want to make)

_____

IV. Give the prospective volunteer a copy of "Volunteer Policies." Following is a copy of those used at Issaquah Villa. These are brief and made for the facility's policy book and inspecting officials, as well as the volunteer, herself.

Volunteer Policies

Volunteers will be utilized at Issaquah Villa in areas of their ability and interest.

They will be scheduled by the department using their services.

A record of hours is to be kept by the department head.

Annual recognition will be scheduled during late May, or in early June, in the form of a tea.

Additional recognition may be instituted as need arises, i.e., pins, or bracelet charms.

A volunteer will be reimbursed for out of pocket costs when doing shopping for a patient or department.

Reimbursement is provided for the volunteer transporting a patient to and from a medical appointment. A schedule is available in the Policy Manual.

V. Give the prospective volunteer a personal copy of "Do's and Don't for Volunteers." Following is a copy of the one used at Issaquah Villa. Remember it is used for all ages. We take time to explain the multiple use feature for simplicity's sake.

Do's & Don'ts for Volunteers

1. Please establish a regular time for volunteering. Be consistent, regular, dependable and on time. If you cannot come in, report by telephone to show that you are faithful to your commitment.

2. If you are sick, or do not feel well, call in. Don't come in unless you are able to work.

3. Be sure you have filled out our Volunteer Information Form so that we will be familiar with your abilities, and know how to reach you. Please make it a point to record your volunteer hours here at the Villa. You make an enormous contribution to our program, which we honor annually.

4. You are entitled to supervision, guidance and orientation from our activity program here at the Villa. Do not roam the home with no direction. Remember you are responsible *for* others and *to* others.

5. Bear in mind at all times that you keep confidential what you see and hear at the Villa. If a resident refers a problem to you, report it to us so that something can be done to solve it—don't attempt to solve it yourself.

6. Do not discuss the Villa with outsiders except in a positive manner. Be a good listener. Do not discuss patients or opinions with outsiders or where patients can hear you. Don't hesitate to say you don't know the answer to a question.

7. Work *with* and not *for* the patients. Initiate and terminate relationships. Be flexible and resourceful. Be impartial.

8. Under no circumstances remove restraints from a patient or take him to the bathroom alone. Report requests of this nature to your volunteer supervisor.

9. Please wear a smile when on duty. Keep your attitude happy and cheerful. This helps our most regressed people to recognize you as a friend. Be sure to avoid using overpowering perfumes. Always use a deodorant.

10. Remember, volunteers are here to aid the residents. Your function is to help with project preparation and activities, to help move residents unable to transport themselves, to give assistance whenever it is needed, and to offer a willing ear without being overly sympathetic. Sympathy is not always the answer to a problem. Avoid emotional involvement. Be objective and impartial, but understanding.

11. Be careful of conversational material you use. Do not volunteer information that could be upsetting to the patient.

12. If residents speak sharply or find fault with you, the staff or their families, do not take it personally. Just remember they cannot vent their frustrations in other ways. Use humor or change the subject. Be enthusiastic and sincere. Look the patient straight in the eye when talking to him.

13. Respect the patients, staff members, your co-workers and rules of the house. Please stand when being introduced to someone; it is a sign of respect and consideration.

14. Do not bring your personal problems to the job.

15. Wear simple clothes and hair style. Try a smock or apron with large pockets to protect your clothing.

16. Be willing to do what you are asked to do. This is an opportunity for growth for you, demanding the best you can give at all times.

17. Be sure you like older, infirm, and sometimes complaining people. They need friendship, love, and understanding from you.

VI. In addition, we have a 3" x 5" card, usually in a color, for each volunteer to carry in her handbag. It lists those qualities to keep constantly in mind—and is useful even when not in the volunteer role.

10 Tips

1. Be on time.
2. Be cheerful.
3. Be dependable; do what you say you'll do.
4. Turn comments into fun and laughter.
5. Smile—all the time.
6. Show respect for everyone.
7. Wear hair in neat style, and simple clothes in good taste.
8. Do not sit on beds, and stand when spoken to.
9. Go more than halfway.
10. Keep busy.

"There is a way to do it better—Find it."

Thomas Edison

VII. Each prospective volunteer is given a copy of our "Waste Materials" list (see page 75) to use himself and to pass along to others. This starts him thinking in terms of practical use for these materials and directs his frame of reference to your needs.

WASTE MATERIALS FOR ISSAQUAH VILLA

OLD NYLON HOSE
CLEAN CLOTH 12" Sq. & LARGER
FELT
RIBBON, RICKRACK, TAPE, LACE
ELASTIC
SPOOLS
PINS, NEEDLES
BUTTONS, BEADS, TRIMS
THREAD, SEWING AND EMBROIDERY
PAPER, ALL KINDS
NAILS, SCREWS
YARN, WOOL OR COTTON
PATTERNS, SIMPLE, FOR APRONS AND STUFFED TOYS
SCRAPS OF WOOD, DOWELING, ETC.
GOOD BOOKS, PAPERBACKS
OLD DOLLS TO RENEW AND DRESS
BINGO PRIZES (KNICKKNACKS, SAMPLES, ETC.)
SALVAGE FROM FACTORIES
TOYS TO REPAIR

VIII. The location of the list of "To Do," which the Activity Program Director makes and keeps up, is pointed out to each volunteer. This is for use if by chance the director is not available during assigned time. On this list we place items such as: projects requiring hand sewing, cutting out projects, threading needles, watering plants, needles, watering plants, enlarging patterns, etc.

IX. A calendar, on 8½" x 11" paper, made by the volunteers, with a 1½" square for each day, is kept posted on the inside of a closet door. In these squares each volunteer records her name and hours for the permanent recognition record. It is their responsibility to be sure the records are kept accurately. The Activity Program Director is responsible for being sure the proper calendar is posted. We usually keep the current month and the future month up simultaneously.

Sun.	Mon.	Tues.	Wed.	Thurs.	Fri.	Sat.
1	2	3	4	5	6	7
8	9	10	11	12	13	14
15	16	17	18	19	20	21
22	23	24	25	26	27	28
29	30	31				

Figure 7-1

This is the extent of our organization and record keeping for volunteers. It is simple, effective, easy to use and based on our program and needs. You can design something similar to fit your needs. Most of it is done ahead of time to form a firm basis for an effective volunteer service program. The truly effective volunteer, realizing our sincere efforts, will feel obligated to do her part in return. There is no substitute for planning ahead, being prepared, and forming a solid basis. Our efforts are repaid many times over. It is part of our responsibility to the volunteer.

Some institutions conduct a formal training session on a set day for a large number of prospective volunteers. We have never done this. It would, no doubt, be easier, but we feel it would not be as individualized and considerate of the volunteer, nor would it utilize the volunteer to her maximum.

There are organizations such as the American Red Cross which train volunteers, but not for any specific facility. This generalized training makes it easier to assimilate them into a new program if they are open-minded and accepting of change.

When a person comes to us all fired up to help, we don't let him lose that spark. We gobble him up, and put him in his niche. Each volunteer has his own training session alone; as alone as you can be in a room with ten or twelve workers, telephone, and interruptions continuously. He gets the idea of how much he is needed to supplement the Activity Program Director's hand right away. And, she has given of her personal time and interest to orient him. This makes a lasting impression and a dependable volunteer.

Our system of training and orientation includes some practical exposure to techniques in handling the aged in the workroom. The formal list of needs of the geriatric person (Section I, Chapter 5) is available to our volunteers at all times.

One other item which may be of help to a newly assigned volunteer is some form of identification. We have tried name tags, badges, smocks, and jumpers. Nothing seemed to click. Finally, we decided upon a smiling face and a helpful attitude, with a verbal identification to the elderly of who we are, and why we are here. It seems to be the answer in our facility. Perhaps it is because we feel more at home, and able, in our own clothing, to prove what we can do.

HOW TO USE VOLUNTEERS

First, the Administrator and the Activity Program Director should decide the role of the volunteer in their facility. A truly successful volunteer program indicates that some very basic planning was done before starting.

The Administrator's Point of View.

1. The Administrator's responsibilities and attitudes toward the volunteer program.
    a. Approval and backing of volunteer program.
    b. Cooperation in the program.
    c. Recognition of staff involvement.
    d. Realization that the volunteer is the ingredient that makes other services tick.
    e. Appointing of volunteer director, with necessary attributes for the job. In our opinion this should be a paid person to insure full dependability on the job.
2. What the Administrator expects and needs from the volunteers.
    a. Willingness to learn and to do what is asked of him as a member of a team.
    b. Dependability, flexibility, impartiality, sense of humor.
    c. Be a good representative to the community.
    d. Be loyal and respect confidences; accept, and understand the older person.
    e. Be accepted by the staff.

Director or Leader of Volunteers—Qualifications.

1. Friendly, warm person.
2. Interested in and likes older people.
3. Generous person, who encourages others to take limelight.
4. Fair person.
5. Honest person, not afraid to say, "I don't know," or "That was my mistake."
6. Humble person, on equal terms with all.
7. Careful person, keeps things in order and doesn't forget promises.
8. Prompt and faithful person.
9. Courageous person.
10. Patient person.
11. Tactful person, who can smooth over sensitive feelings.
12. Humorous person.
13. Willing to try new ideas.
14. Relaxed person.
15. Mediator, peacemaker.
16. Planner, one who makes things happen.

The selection of the proper kind of person for this position has a great deal to do with whether the volunteer is dependable, enjoys her work, and is productive.

Volunteer Director's Needs.

What the Volunteer Director expects and needs from the volunteer: Dependability to help with:

a. Transportation, appointments, and on call.
b. Errands for department and senior citizens, inside and outside of facility.
c. Arts and crafts program.
d. Visiting, reading, letter writing.
e. Assignment to an individual as a personal volunteer.
f. As a technical specialist contributing talent.
g. To provide special activity, weekly or monthly.
h. To help daily with tea, coffee, films.

Senior Citizen's Needs.

What the senior citizen expects and needs from the volunteer are:

a. Tolerance and understanding.
b. Complete and individual attention.
c. Honesty and friendliness.
d. Sincerity and courtesy.
e. Assistance in activity.
f. Praise and recognition for effort put forth.

Volunteer's Needs

What the volunteer expects and needs from giving her time, interest, and abilities are:

a. A good supervisor, who will treat her as a co-worker, give her firm direction, and guidance.
b. A regular assignment in the program, geared to her education, interest, experience, and temperament.
c. Knowledge of the organization, its policies, personnel, and program schedule.
d. Location of rooms, supplies, and utilities.
e. Respect for her opinions, ideas and suggestions.
f. Support and cooperation of the whole staff.
g. A safe place to leave her personal belongings.
h. An adequate place in which to carry on her assigned job.
i. Recognition of her efforts through expressions of appreciation.

Volunteens

Volunteens are very little different from adult volunteers. They have all of the same personal differences and assimilation problems. They are likely to be more boisterous, ask more questions, and be somewhat more demanding of their supervisor. They are curious, want to be of help and learn. We have found that two of these energetic and enthusiastic young people is all we can handle at one time.

Volunteens can be taught to do anything. Their eagerness to learn is all-consuming. If they are not this kind of child, and you, as their supervisor did not pick it up at the start, they will soon drop out of their own accord. During the personal interview it is hard to tell genuine enthusiasm for temporary, because of the excitement of trying something new, and because you want to give each one a chance. Also, do not underrate the influence of a successful pal. Beware of taking daughters of your best adult volunteers. They may not work out, and you could lose two.

Try to group teens who like each other. Usually this is no problem. There is a happy medium between the eager beaver who is on the go every minute, hard to settle down to a steady pace—and the quiet, shy child who must be guided every step. Both are hard to turn into helpful workers. Look for the happy medium in all volunteers: eager, but willing to listen; enthusiastic and imaginative, but willing to be moulded and tempered; thinking and using common sense, but also anxious to add her ideas to the pool. They do take more time in planning and guiding than adult volunteers, but their freshenss adds something to the program and their eagerness is appreciated by the elderly. Older people like young people who are sincere. As one elderly person said, "These lovely young girls helping and just being around make such a difference in our day."

This group presents a new approach for the supervisor. Be sure you like and enjoy working with this age and stage of learning. If you don't, steer clear of the volunteens.

This list is just a start of the many jobs our volunteers do for senior citizens under guidance and supervision: errands, mail delivery, letter writing—(we check spelling and address), reading, conversing, mending, entertaining with musical instruments, singing, dancing puppets, serving tea, conducting games, manicures, craft preparation and completion, adopting a grandparent to serve, addressing mass mailings, operating mimeo machine, making decorations, serving parties, watering plants and arranging flowers. This can go on and on as the situation presents itself. Be prepared to have something ready on a moment's notice for them to pick and do.

Adult volunteers, since they have learned advanced skills and techniques, drive cars and have outside contacts, can be used in additional ways. Adults can:

- Arrange for and conduct special game sessions: bingo, shuffleboard, ring toss, etc.
- Do cutting and sewing of projects.
- Conduct special parties, including decorations, entertainment, and program.
- Show films and slides.
- Run errands and do shopping for occupational therapy department, activity program, and senior citizens who have no families.
- Provide homemade goodies and serve them at parties.
- Arrange extensive musical programs, on a regular basis, such as Sunday afternoon music.
- Conduct discussion groups.
- Transport the elderly to appointments, shopping, and community affairs, museums and zoos.
- Provide rides at holiday times.
- Register senior citizens to vote, and securing absentee ballots.
- Invite local groups to entertain.
- Have white elephant drives for game prizes.
- Collect coupons and send for premiums.
- Meet family members at bus.
- Bring old fashioned exhibits—cars, dolls, etc.

No matter who does all of these things, he becomes your volunteer; helpful to your program without a great deal of training on your part. Just a phone call in most cases, and some rearranging of furniture to accomodate them, is all that is necessary.

HOW TO KEEP THEM

It takes only a few principles to keep good volunteers:

1. *Communicate with them.* This starts at the personal interview. Take time to listen to them, answer their questions, assimilate their good ideas into the program. Let them have the spotlight. Stress their good points.
2. *Keep their schedule open for them.* Be considerate and notify them of changes well ahead of time if there is to be an interruption in the regular schedule.
3. *Be sure the volunteers are familiar with the fact that their actions do not precipitate peculiar characteristics of the elderly, such as:*

- Fear of change
- Tiring easily
- Craving for individual attention and tender, loving care
- Having periods of depression and mood swings
- Having feelings close to the surface, and being sensitive
- Showing competition among themselves
- Enjoying repeated talk of the past
- Dwelling on their physical ailments
- Having memory lapses

4. *Make the volunteers aware that these problems in handling the senior citizen may be encountered at any time, with very little stimulus:*
   - Rudeness
   - Jealousies
   - Seating arguments
   - The dominating individual
   - The uninvited guest
   - Newcomer's need for attention

5. *Recognize their efforts.* Determine a number of service hours for material recognition, such as, 30 service hours for one year. Thank them with personal notes and telephone calls. Praise them publicly in your newsletter and local newspapers. Arrange an annual day of recognition for granting awards. A tea or luncheon means a great deal to the volunteers. Material recognition can take the form of a pin or certificate. At Issaquah Villa we have awarded, for the first year, a gold bracelet with a heart charm. Each successive year an additional charm is given. Be sure contributions to your program do not go unnoticed.

Summary

Remember that each smiling face, every extra sign of friendship, every errand run, every tray favor or May basket, cannot be purchased with money. It is all due to devotion and love on the part of your volunteers. They make the day more meaningful to someone who might otherwise have felt left out and forgotten. For this giving of themselves, find endless ways to thank them.

Chapter 8

HANDLING SPECIAL NEEDS
OF PARTICULAR PEOPLE

Every senior citizen is an individual with very special needs. He has grown that way year after year, as the currents of life have buffeted him this way and that. There are always reasons why he is the "loner," the sidewalk superintendent," or the "I-can't-do-it" guy, the "I-don't-want-to-try-it-right-now" guy, or the cock-sure "I'm-always-right" guy. The reasons may not be obvious, and they may be devious—sometimes physical, sometimes mental, sometimes emotional, and sometimes all three. You may not be able to tell by looking at him what special needs he has. But, by association and observation of his sensory output, his physical and mental motivation, his ability to understand, to respond, to participate and react to you and to others, you'll begin to figure out where his needs lie.

A very special need of some patients is to be left alone, at least by other patients. Although he resists all socializing, he needs someone with a pleasant manner, relaxed attitude, and compassionate countenance to listen to his desires and his frustrations. He really doesn't want to be alone, but he is frightened and needs encouragement in breaking down the barrier.

Another person may need to be kept busy, but have no desire to rub elbows with her fellow residents. Her special need is to be allowed to work where and how she wishes until she takes the initiative, or you have aroused the curiosity in her, to want to join the others. This takes weeks of patience on the part of the staff, and some carefully worded hint dropping about activities going on in other parts of the facility.

There is the person who needs a place to fuss and be creative at any hour of the day. She may want to make rather useless articles, which seem to be a waste of time, effort, and material, but this type of activity is constructive for this type of person. She finds great pleasure, satisfaction, and happiness in her chosen pastime. And there are always people who appreciate and want the resulting article.

In many cases, the senior citizen who keeps himself busy is the one with the best health and the least problems.

If you, as an Activity Program Director, have access to background material, such as talks with family members, written life history, or medical charts, these will provide some actual and determined facts about the resident. If you do not have any of these sources open to you, talk with the nurse and spend lots of time getting acquainted with the person yourself. At least find out what his vocation was, his avocation is, where his interests lie, and what his abilities are.

SENILITY

This is a broad term which means growing old, with slowing and deterioration in physical prowess, mental activity, and emotional stability. It is usually associated with the elderly, but this process knows no chronological age. Generalized aging starts when we are born and progresses with us. In some people it moves faster than in others.

Senile people are pitiful, at times seemingly lost and at other times sadly realizing their deteriorating abilities. Because of this, they seem helpless and hopeless. There actually are no hopeless people, only hopeless situations in which they find themselves, and perhaps you can help here.

This type of person is very responsive to affection, touching, warmth, sensitive to moods, and is sometimes affected by atmospheric pressures and changes. Your undivided attention, friendliness, and sincerity, are basic needs for them. Always leave them with some encouraging feeling. Never let them fail, at least in their estimation. Work it out so that they succeed. They will always have excuses as to why "they cannot do it," "won't try," "maybe later," or "not anymore." Here is where you give and they respond. Interest them in someone else, something in their surroundings, talk about something they remember, bring a flower to a former gardener, wool cards and wool to Swedish lady, or even a spinning wheel for her to try out.

However, be careful in renewing old skills. Don't let them do poorly what they once did well. This could be very discouraging to them and a set-back in your efforts. Adapt and show them how you will make use of their products.

THE CONFUSED PERSON

The confused person may be senile also, but not always. One thing this person almost always knows is his name. You may have to try several forms, even a maiden name, or Mr., or a nickname to get the response you want. He may be disoriented as to where he is or how old he is, and he may be out of contact with the time of day, or season, or the year. He may be able to recall early life happenings, but not remember that he has just finished breakfast or that his wife died six months ago. He may cry and whine a lot because he is unhappy. Logic may only tend to make matters worse. A 96 year old will say, "I saw my mother get out of that car. Why doesn't she come in?" To assure him his mother is not there, and is probably dead, only makes him more sure you are wrong and that he is being deceived. To distract his attention may be of some help here.

This state of mind can be caused by many illnesses and deterioration processes, by emotional disturbances and brain damage. It is a condition commonly faced when working in the geriatric field. Some days it is worse than others, but these people still have their five senses. They can *smell* aromas, although sometimes they are unable to identify the fragrance. Their fingers *feel* textures. Their eyes *see* line and color, but perhaps not as perfectly as you do. Their ears *hear* sounds, and noises are likely to frighten them. They can usually *taste* different foods, and let you know what they like, but may not be able to identify the taste. They sometimes have an intangible *sixth* sense, which can startle you. It can be an uncanny observation about you or another person, or a generalization that is so realistic it strikes home. Pick out the good and active qualities of the elderly. Stimulate their senses.

In order to be an effective worker with this type of senior citizen, a calm, quiet, pleasant person, with a dignified and slow-paced manner is necessary. Her motions should not be quick and jerky, this will startle them. Her quiet, listening way will soothe them. Her encouraging attitude will get the best results with them.

The following suggestions have value in working with the confused and disoriented person:

- *Interesting cloth books, with pages that "work" and have many textures.* These can be constructed in a similar manner to the books for children. Cloth pages with a zipper that zips, pockets which button and unbutton, and pockets which have articles in them to be pulled out. A long string, securely fastened, will have buttons or beads, spool or whistle to be taken out, and when investigated completely, tucked back inside. Snaps can fasten the ears in place on a clown's face, or a hook and eye will fasten the door of a teepee closed. An animal cut from a deep pile fabric will be good to feel. Familiar objects, such as a teapot or hammer, can be outlined with tape to be followed by a finger.

- *Pillow, inside of pillow, inside of pillow, from large to small.* The smallest pillow is the only one stuffed and completely closed on all four, six, or eight sides. Each successive pillow has a different type of closure. Try zippers, snaps, hooks and eyes, and even Velcro. Stuff the smallest inside the next largest, and close. Continue this process in assembling the one large pillow. The elderly person will get the most fun out of taking it apart. Putting it together may not be as exciting a pastime as trying to figure out "What is inside the pillow?" There are endless possibilites here. Many kinds of fabrics with texture, or pictures appliqued which are easily recognizable, tassels, cords, and decorations made with buttons are all good. Try having an alert senior citizen make these for the less able.

- *Treasure chests of familiar items to unpack and repack.* A good way to arouse interest in something like this is to say, "Please hold this for me for a minute," or "Take care of this for me." Place in the lap of someone who needs something to do. Pretty soon, as you go about helping others, curiosity has won and the box is open. This same technique can be used in a conversation group where items are discussed as they are brought forth. This stimulates experience patterns in older minds.

- *Bean bags made in odd shapes, such as frogs or turtles.* These can be fun to toss back and forth; especially if they have a bell on them, or in them, with the dry, noisy beans. They are easy to catch and are easy on the skin if dropped.

- *Activity apron.* This is like a butcher apron with large pockets. This can be tied onto the person who will pull items out of the pockets. Items can be fastened in the pockets with shoe laces, and can consist of a change purse or wallet, pencil and pad of paper, long ribbon for tying bows, small soft toy, or other familiar items.

- *Repetitive projects.* Examples are listed below:
  —Pompom animals
  —Cutting squares and sewing together for afghans and pillows
  —Winding skein dolls
  —Hooking small pieces for pillow tops

—Pulling threads in coarse cloth and running yarn through
—Tearing paper to use in mache process
—Crochet single chains
—Braiding
—Stuffing toy animals
—Stringing spools
—Cutting nylons for stuffing
—Pomander balls

● *Collect together several fragrances.* You can use a rose, perfume, cinnamon, oil of cloves, honey, grated onion, dried lavender, balsam. See if they can identify the odors, or if the fragrances conjure up any old memories.

● *Cautions:*
    —Avoid using electric or mechanical machines or tools in which a finger might be injured.
    —Avoid sharp and pointed tools. Use blunt scissors.
    —Avoid fine, small, and dark materials. Keep things bright, large, and simple.
    —Avoid using non-drinkable liquids and non-edible materials.

Currently of interest for people working with the confused and disoriented person is the subject of remotivation. The aims in this technique are to remotivate the elderly to take a renewed interest in their surroundings by focusing their attention upon the simple objective features of everyday life that are related to their emotional difficulties. Printed materials, courses in techniques, and films are available through:

> Remotivation Project
> Smith, Klein and French Laboratories
> 1500 Spring Garden St.
> Philadelphia, Pa., 19101

THE STROKE OR CEREBRAL VASCULAR ACCIDENT VICTIM

In the late 1920's, my grandparents referred to what we now call a stroke as a "shock." Indeed it was, and still is, to the person experiencing it, and it is also a considerable blow to the family involved.

Two of the main causes of a stroke or Cerebral Vascular Accident are: a break in a blood vessel in the brain, allowing blood to escape into the tissues; and, the formation of a blood clot which blocks a blood vessel in the brain. Depending upon the location of the clot or break, the result of this accident can be severe or mild. It can paralyze one whole side of the body, the speech mechanism, the brain's ability to understand, and, as with any illness, the ability to think clearly may be impaired. All of the senses, and perception, may also be affected. It is easy to have a defeatist attitude toward recovery when so many vital abilities are suddenly lost. Some people make a remarkable recovery from a stroke and others are disabled for life, depending upon the location and severity of the accident. Inborn personality, drive, and determination, play a large part in the recovery. Many stroke victims live on for years after being disabled.

It is the responsibility of the people around a stroke victim to encourage and help in every way possible. The physician will start corrective measures soon after the onset. From an activity point of view, we must remember to deal first with a whole person who just happens to be a stroke victim. He is overly conscious of himself and his future. His attitudes of self-concern dominate his thoughts, his limited energy, and all of his time. He may cry and show extreme periods of depression. Do not reflect an attitude of hopelessness. Be encouraging, give lots of patience, help, and guidance toward developing his own new ways. This attitude on your part will lead him toward future independence.

Three important needs must be faced by all concerned with his immediate care:

1. *Adequate rest.*
   He is weak, lacks vitality, and tires quickly. His body must be in a supporting position during rest periods.
2. *Appropriate nutrition.*
   At first he must be helped to eat or be fed. His impaired judgment affects the when and the what of his meals, so guidance is necessary.
3. *Re-establishing acceptable personal habits and toiletry.*
   Efforts in this area should be attempted at his peak of energy, which is in the morning, and for a very short period of time at first. This training will take a long time, lots of help, and patience. In order to direct his undivided attention toward these efforts, eliminate disorderliness and bright colors from the treatment area. Small things are distracting and he may not be able to verbalize what is bothering him. Do not try to do any intellectual or mind-training work after a strenuous physical therapy or muscle training session.

This particular type of patient can be helped greatly if the Activity Program Director happens to be a Registered Occupational Therapist. She can contribute her abilities early in the retraining process for activities of daily living, splinting, adapting eating and dressing devices, instructing in their use, and designing individualized appliances.

Communication is essential between the patient, and all personnel concerned with his care. Develop a sign language, if necessary, with the patient. Nodding or shaking of the head for "yes" and "no" or simply closing of eyes for "yes." Encourage the patient to work hard himself.

Examples of Individual Appliances for Stroke Victims

Hand expander. Normally the muscles which bend and flex the fingers, wrist, and elbow (also ankle, knee, and hip) are stronger than the ones which straighten or extend these same joints. In a stroke, the extending muscles are weakened and so the flexing muscles tend to pull the hand and fingers into a grip-like position. In order to keep the fingers somewhat open and the nails from digging into the palm, you can make what I call a hand expander: (Figure 8-1)

- 1 empty pill bottle about 1" in diameter, 2¼" -3" long (remove lid)
- Cut a 9" piece of ¾" webbing
- Cut a 1" patch of Velcro and separate the parts (hook and loop)
- Stitch this patch of Velcro, the loop piece on one end of the webbing facing upwards, and the hook piece in the other end facing downwards.
- Using masking or adhesive tape in a wrapping motion around the bottle, fasten this piece of webbing to the outside of the bottle along one side.
- Place the bottle in the open palm of the hand and wrap the webbing over the back of the hand, fastening it in place by pressing together the two patches of Velcro.

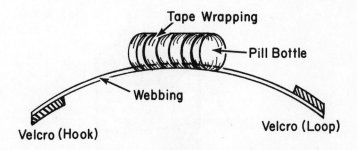

Figure 8-1

Devices to Encourage Self-care and Independence in Eating:

Built-up handles: These can be made for the spoon first, and later for the fork, when hand coordination becomes better. This same procedure can be used on pencils and pens for re-education in writing. (Figure 8-2)

- Cut a 1" thick piece of foam rubber to the proper size for type of tool and size of grip. Be sure it overlaps about 1" around.
- Stick a piece of ¾" wide masking tape, 4" longer than the width of the foam rubber, onto the rubber close to one end, so that a 2" length of tape protrudes on each side.
- Roll the foam rubber lengthwise with the tape inside to provide a smooth area for the utensil to slide in and out. The 2" pieces of tape fold over to fasten the roll at the open ends. Run a piece of tape around the center exterior of the roll also.

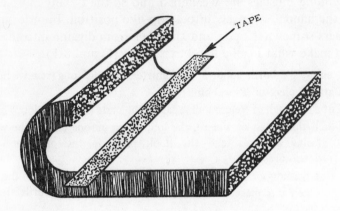

BUILD UP FOR HANDLES

Figure 8-2

Commercial eating aids: These are available in many types. We have used successfully the suction cup holder and Plate Guard combination. There are many styles of special spoons and forks, and combination tools for eating. The suction cup holder immobilizes the plate in one position (wet it before adhering it between table and plate); while the Plate Guard forms a fence against which the food is pushed onto the utensil.

In an emergency, a wet wash cloth or towel placed under the plate or bowl will keep it from sliding while the patient is trying to get the food onto the spoon or fork. Additional help in food preparation by cutting is usually necessary.

Stimulants for the poor appetite.

For the patient who has little interest in eating, you can try several things. Perhaps it is a medication which is affecting the appetite, or the paralysis of one side of the face. First of all, talk it over with the patient and try to find out what he thinks is bothering him. Then use a little psychology in choosing favorite foods and serving them in a style which he will appreciate. Perhaps you could use a pretty china plate, real silver utensils, or a cloth napkin. Something from home may help. Taking the food off the tray, or adding a vase of small flowers, which may be kept after the meal is over, may stimulate the desire to eat.

Protection for the patient's clothing may be needed. A good-sized bib, made of absorbent material, tied well up around the neck, will encourage him to eat independently. All evidence of spillage will be removed after the meal. This is a must for all patients who lack manual and upper extremity coordination. He is sensitive about his messiness, but will improve only by use and exercise in this direction.

One-Handers.

Since many stroke victims lose the use of one hand, the following suggestions and devices for one-handers will be most applicable:

A patient with a paralyzed hand, whether or not it is his dominant hand, has an emotional problem as well as a physical one. If the paralysis is of long duration, the objective of involving the patient into the activity program is made more difficult physically, emotionally, and socially. For the patient has already set his mind to certain standards, and usually it is: "I can't do anything with only one hand." If the loss of the use of the hand is of recent origin, there is a much greater possibility that the patient will be encouraged to make use of the remaining functions. Here the Physical Therapist and the Occupational Therapist are valuable in restoring as much use as possible through prescribed exercises and activities.

The Activity Director must discourage the patient's normal reaction of, "I don't have two hands, so I won't try to do anything." She must encourage the attitude of, "Let's see how much I can do with one good hand," using also what ability remains in the affected hand. At this point confidence is built with praise and gradual success. Be sure the patient has success and sees progress in some form each day. This may be difficult at times for the Activity Director, for this feeling results almost wholly from the way in which she handles situations.

In choosing a project for such a patient, be sure it is a useable item, which can be accomplished successfully with the ability available. Do not offer this patient a task too fine for his grasp, manual dexterity, or eyesight. These skills are all affected and involved in his efforts. Keep the activities large and of the type which do not demand perfection of detail. For example, choose a fabric of burlap texture rather than fine cotton, and use rug yarns with plastic needles rather than two-ply wool with metal needles. Be sure that the patient is familiar with the process in the beginning. There would be nothing more frustrating to a patient than to try to learn a new technique at the same time as learning new methods of using his hands. For example, don't try to teach a patient to knit with one hand, if he had never knitted previously.

The following are some suggestions of mechanical substitutes and aids for the person with only one good hand:

Stabilizing:

- *Masking tape* for fastening writing paper, bingo cards, cloth to table, patterns to cloth; make loop of tape with sticky side out and place between cloth and pattern.
- *Rubber suction cups* for fastening down plates and bowls. There are several sizes and styles. Also for fastening down nail brush for washing hands. (Screw suction cups to back of brush and adhere to bowl.)
- *Weights.* Use weak hand as stabilizer. Bag weights may be made in different sizes and shapes in unbleached cotton cloth, filled with lead wheel balancing weights, sand, beans, or rice.
- *Clips,* the pinch together type, for lightweight items.
- *"C" clamps* for fastening looms, woodworking, weaving frames, down to a firm surface. Also embroidery hoops (see aids for sewing).

- *Large spring clamps* of metal, like clothes pins—available from Sears-Roebuck & Company.
- *Clothes pins* for fastening books and magazines open.
- *Clip boards* for fastening paper, directions and patterns firmly.
- *Fly-tying vise* for holding crochet and knitting
- *Small vise* for holding crochet and knitting needles. (Use foam rubber between vise and needle to keep needle from revolving.)
- *Magnets on metal*, must be very strong magnets.
- *Paper for cutting*. Let paper protrude from the middle of a thick book, and use bent handled scissors.

Aids for one-handed sewing:

- *Needle threading*. Stick needle into cork or styrofoam or pincushion, then thread. Or, use commercial needle threader.
- *Holding sewing for working*. Stabilize work to arm of chair or table, fasten other end to waist, or weight it in lap.
- *Braiding*. Use old fashioned braiding bird or clamp fastened to firm surface.
- *Cutting cloth*. Use masking tape to fasten cloth to table, cut pattern out of sand paper and use sand side down. (This eliminates use of pins.) Use bent handled scissors.
- *Embroidering*. Clamp hoop to table by using a "C" clamp and a thin strip of wood or metal across the hoop (under the clamp). A tongue blade will work.
- *Ironing*. Guide iron direction with good forearm on handle. Good hand is used ahead of iron, spreading and smoothing material. Care not to burn fingers on the iron.
- *Painting*. Fasten object to be painted with a weight inside. Or, make a corner brace to push it against for stability. Fasten down stretched canvas or paper with proper mechanical aid, to a firm surface.
- *Playing card holder*. Use empty, closed cigarette carton with a piece of 2"x 4" inside for weight. Tape ends closed and stick cards between lid flap and side of carton.
- *Magnetic retriever*. This can be used for picking up metal objects such as nails, screws, drills, knitting needles, crochet hooks, pins, and needles. There are also many types of commercial grippers with tong ends. This is also useful for a wheelchair patient. (Figure 8-3)

A simple, long-handled hook can be made by bending the shoulder part of a coat hanger length-wise. (Figure 8-4)

Pressure cans with push buttons to operate are a boon to one-handers. Almost everything comes packaged in them today, from food to paint.

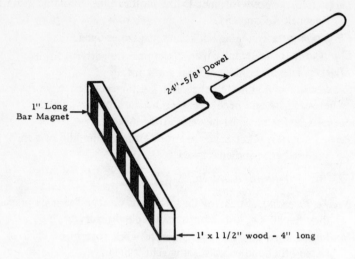

1" Long
Bar Magnet

24"-5/8' Dowel

←— 1' x 1 1/2" wood - 4" long

Figure 8-3

Figure 8-4

In the personal care area, many techniques may be used to adapt combs, shoehorns, shavers, toothbrushes, etc., to specific needs and uses. Attaching long handles or elastic band holders are two suggestions, and many catalogues illustrate commercial adaptations available. Use a little ingenuity and put yourself in the patient's shoes to solve a problem. Anything you can do to help the patient to independence will help the staff and family as well.

WHEEL CHAIR BOUND PATIENTS

Weights can be added to the backs of wheel chairs to balance the heavy patient who leans forward. A double leg amputee needs weights on the front to counteract the loss of limb weight. These weights can be made with dry sand or with broken and discarded auto wheel balancing weights. The chosen filling should be sewn into a heavy plastic bag, which in turn is sewn into a canvas outer bag.

Finished size should not exceet 6" square. Machine stitch, firmly to the bag, two 24" ties of webbing, for fastening them to the chair. The weight can be from 5 to 8 lbs.

Lapboards

The simpler it is the better the design. Proportions should be about 2' x 3' or 21" x 32". Masonite or plywood may be used, with two good sides, cut with rounded corners and a body-contoured section 18" long and 8" deep at the widest point. It can be sanded and finished on both sides with a plastic finish; or it can have a vinyl cover glued to one side. Even contact paper will give a good surface which can be replaced easily. Drill two holes at the back corners, which will accomodate the fastening ropes. Made this way it is reversible; one side for eating and one side for working. If the patient's coordination is so poor that the lap tray does not stay in place, but slides to one side, cleats may be needed on the under side, screwed to the board at a point outside the chair arms. (Dotted lines on drawing.)

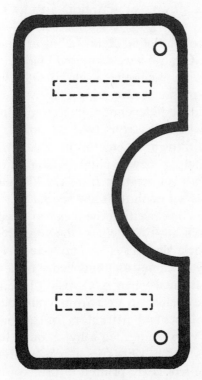

Figure 8-5

DEFECTS IN VISION, SPEECH, AND HEARING

These three senses are very often impaired in the older person. Difficulty in seeing, talking, and hearing, can be caused at any age, by illnesses and accidents; but with older people sometimes it is caused by just growing old.

Vision Defects

For the visually limited there are numerous private and public agencies now concerned with providing helpful aids. Talking Book Machines and Magnetic Tape Players are available free. These are provided by the United States Government and available through your local library for the blind. Also provided are the recordings to be used with them. Large print books, magazines, and newspapers are now produced by publishers and organizations with the visually limited person in mind. These are available through your local library and bookmobile. *The New York Times,* large print edition, published weekly, is sold on private subscription. *Reader's Digest* has a large print edition also.

Institutions for the blind are installing architectural innovations to help the blind. One we have seen used in a geriatric health facility involved handrails on the walls. Each corridor had its individually shaped hand rail—round, square, triangular, with grooves. These were helpful for individual independence; after preliminary instruction, one would know where he was by feel.

The Activity Program Director in a geriatric facility may be called upon to help a newly blind person gain independence in eating. This involves cooperation from the kitchen. The individual's food plate must be set up in the same special way for each meal. For example, have the cook position the meat on the plate at 12 o'clock, the potato or starch at 3:00 o'clock, the vegetable at 6 o'clock, and the salad at 9 o'clock. Have a system and have everyone stick to it.

The counting of money and knowledge of denominations is also something to be learned when one's vision is limited. Help for this type of need is available to you from your local Society for the Blind. They have classes and instructors for such needs.

At Issaquah Villa we needed a hymn book for our older people who could not see the words in a regular hymn book. So, we designed one. The words are printed in primary capitals, one hymn to a page, and mimeographed. The washable binders hold not only hymns, but a Christmas Carol section and one of old time songs. The music counterpart to the hymn book, which has only music, has been made in duplicate and is kept at the piano. There is a song book called, "Let's Sing" in large print, which is available from St. Otto's Home, Little Falls, Minnesota, 56345.

Addresses for Help with the Blind

American Foundation for the Blind, Inc.
   15 W. 16th St., New York, N.Y., 10011
American Brotherhood for the Blind, Inc.
   P.O. Box 500, Nashua, New Hampshire
Association of Hospital & Institution Libraries
   50 E. Huron St., Chicago, Illinois
   (List of reading aids for the handicapped)
Xerox Corporation
   P.O. Box 24, Rochester, N.Y., 14601
   (large type books and periodicals)
New York Times
   Times Square, N.Y., N.Y., 10036
   (Large type weekly edition)
New England Council of Optometrists, Inc.
   101 Tremont St., Boston, Mass.
National Aid to Visually Handicapped
   3201 Balboa St., San Francisco, Calif., 94121

Speech Defects

A speech defect can be very frustrating, especially if the person can understand and yet cannot respond verbally.

Causes and types of aphasia, the loss of power to use words, are numerous, and the study and treatment of this impairment is a complete science. For help in this area, a speech therapist should be consulted.

The following is a good example of why the Activity Director needs to have some knowledge about the background of a person:

One day the R.N. came to the Activity Director, asking if she could come to see what she thought could be done to help a newly admitted patient feed himself. As the Activity Director and the nurse walked to the patient's room, the Activity Director learned the patient's name and some facts. His behavior had been socially unacceptable, with the use of loud unintelligible words and flailing of arms and legs. He was a stroke victim, but of a mild form as far as physical impairment. His damage had reduced his ability to express himself with intelligible words, and thus be understood. This made him irritable and frustrated. The Activity Director approached him with a smile and an eager, "Good morning, Tom." The words which followed had the sound of Spanish, then Swedish, but no English. "Tom, su hablo Espanol?" "Ah, si, uno doce tres—." Then, he was off, with more double talk, which is exactly what it sounded like.

At this time he was unable to hold a spoon. Even if he could, his coordination was so impaired that he did not know where his mouth was. In two days time, with concentrated help in adaptive equipment, coordination of the direction of his arm, and a few Spanish words, his physical coordination in both arms and legs was rapidly returning. His ability to make judgments, pay attention, and control his physical behavior also showed rapid improvement. However, he was not able to do much better at speech. A speech therapist was called in and the family supplied the information that Tom spoke a little of several languages, since he was a seaman for many years. Also, since most of his foreign words were of the profane variety, this accounted for the loudness and physical gestures.

After a few weeks of help from the speech therapist, Tom was speaking at least clearly enough to be understood, and was able to go home. This shows how closely related all of the senses are.

Defects in Hearing

Loss of hearing, in any degree, can result in emotional problems for a person. Mental ideation can develop, and cause psychiatric symptoms. Since the deaf person cannot hear what is said, he may feel people are talking about him. Most older people tend to mumble, and to not move their lips in enunciating words. Dentures can add to this problem. So, not to be able to hear what a person is saying, or in a not too clear manner, is likely to cause frustration, misunderstanding, and anger. The result can be warped and strained personality traits. To be totally deaf is a serious handicap and creates a lonesome world for the victim.

Communication can take several forms:

- *Written:* Always carry paper and pencil for your use and that of the elderly. Write or print carefully.

- *Signs:* Facial, hand, and body motions can supplement vocal sounds.

- *Lip Reading:* This science is taught by societies for the hard of hearing all over the nation, and should be started before the hearing fails completely.

● *Hearing Aids:* There are many kinds, and they are usually fairly expensive. Testing for the proper one for the problem can be done by the local hard of hearing society, or hearing and speech center. It is a good idea for the Activity Director to be familiar with battery types, and installation of them in the more common types of hearing aids. Individual hearing aid representatives will answer questions about operation and maintenance of their product. They will even come for instruction and familiarization sessions.

Summary

In summary, we cannot stress too often that a happy expression on your face, a warmth in your manner, and a sincere interest in the senior citizen, will pay off in better relations with those people for whom you have a responsibility toward bringing happiness during their later years. A truly eager, interested, and creative Activity Program Director will go on from here and develop many additional ideas for helping with the special needs for particular people and seeking help where it is needed.

Section II

PARTIES, HOLIDAYS, AND OTHER ENTERTAINMENT

Chapter 9

INVOLVING EVERYONE
IN A GOOD TIME

"Sweet recreation barr'd, what doth insure
But moody and dull melancholy?"

Shakespeare, *Comedy of Errors*

(Act V, Scene I)

Since this part of the activity program involves the use of volunteers and other outside help, and has a definite public relations aspect, our suggestions will be made with this in mind.

PARTIES

To an elderly person, a party is any deviation from the dull, the usual, the routine. A party can be planned for those portions of the day and evening when there is time, due to lack of responsibilities elsewhere, to sit, to take part, and to enjoy the "doings." Senior citizens like to be included in the plans of when, where, who, what and why. They want to know everything and every detail. If they are being surprised, they feel they are missing part of the party for they've not had time to get themsleves into the mood and frame of mind necessary to absorb every second. So give them at least a short notice.

It's a good idea to have a standard schedule of parties such as a regular birthday party, weekly bingo parties and special holiday parties. But don't let this early scheduling become so necessary to planning that an impromptu party cannot be enjoyed. A party can be held anywhere, at any time if the ingredients are there. The ingredients which make parties successful for the elderly would fall like lead balloons for any other age.

Suppose the weatherman says it's going to be a lovely warm afternoon and you repeat this to a patient. "Let's have tea on the patio," is the comment. Take the cue and make the tea a little different. Bring Gus, who plays the accordian, out of doors to create an atmosphere, or perhaps one of your music volunteers would be able to come on a moment's notice with her autoharp to sing. Don't forget employees have talents too. Maybe an aide can whistle, really whistle a tune, to create a light hearted and happy mood. On your lunch hour, go to the store for a different treat: pretzels, English biscuits or fruit. With regular crackers for those whose digestions are touchy, one of these additions, the change of location and the music, would make a party. At least call it one. Plan for stability and enjoyment, but keep yourself and party times flexible.

In setting these party hours, consider the other department's schedules, so that personnel can be included. Usually just before the shift change in the afternoon, there's an opportunity for the staff to stop a minute to see what's going on. Again just after lunch or supper, and before bed time there are pauses. So these are good hours for you to choose for your parties. These hours seem to be less full for the elderly. Late in the day is not considered the peak energy period for any senior citizen. That comes in the mornings and at least before 3 P.M. So these afternoon and evening party times require the use of helpers or volunteers to make the party successful.

It may be a consideration, in a hospital setting, to have special parties, such as individual birthday parties, at meal time, when food is the subject of the moment anyway. Be flexible and open to new suggestions and ideas.

Necessary ingredients for an enjoyable party are:

(1) Communication. Notices, signs and talking it up will let them know what is going to go on, where it will go on, who will put it on, when it will go on and also why. Is it a birthday, a holiday, or a "just because" day party? Or perhaps the birthday is planned because a volunteer or a family member wants to exercise an ability or practice a talent. Perhaps a recent bride will come in her gown to walk the halls to the wedding music once again. The latter calls for tall white cake and the party is on.

(2) Entertainment. This can be music, a juggler, an art show, an old toy exhibit with trains that run along the floor, a magician, dancing, singing, old dolls and, the favorites, films and slides. Ideas are endless. A dog obedience demonstration, held out of doors on a nice day or a visit of an old car or fire engine would hit the spot.

(3) Be aware of the physical needs of your entertainment and volunteers. Arrange for space to dance, walls on which to hang pictures, tables for

displays, a piano well tuned and clean, room to change costumes. Present one activity at a time; not too many things to think about at once. Avoid a three-ring circus atmosphere. The excitement of one ring is all the older people can enjoy. A little goes a long way and is relished more and longer than too much. If you are planning an exhibit or art display, allow space between items so that each unit can be an entity within itself. Older people tend to see a line of unfamiliar objects as a blur since their eyes are not as strong as they once were. A lot of effort goes into these affairs, so be sure they can be enjoyed by the senior citizens.

(4) Food. To the senior citizen, this is the main ingredient of any party. They want something different to eat, especially if the party is for an instituionalized group. Volunteers and the elderly will help with it, but you need to spark it with suggestions. Provide ideas. Suggest cakes, in unusual shapes or styles; cupcakes, plain or decorated; doughnut holes or pretzels. Serve them in an unusual method, such as wrabbing them hobo style in a napkin, with a beverage. Don't forget the candles an any birthday cake. If you have a group of physically well people, perhaps they would like popcorn, old fashioned hand turned ice cream in cones, or a foreign type of food for a change. Perhaps they would like to have a hand in making and serving their own treats.

Working out the details of a party can be lots of fun. If the elderly are capable and able to form a committee to plan their own party, you sit in and keep the ball rolling with practical ideas. Perhaps a community group wants to arrange a party. By all means keep your group in a position of acceptance of these outside ideas and help.

For any party, start the preparations well ahead by making a list of items or symbols which have to do with the theme or holiday. For instance, choose a patriotic theme for the Fourth of July. On your list would be: drums, flags, parades, firecrackers, cannon, picnics, hot weather, watermelon, red, white and blue. Fit as many of these as you can into the party plan in the form of favors, food, place-mats and decorations.

The same technique can be used for any holiday or theme. A highlight of the year could be a fish barbeque. Perhaps a fishing group had a big catch and wish to share it with your group. If not, hot dogs taste good done on an outdoor grill.

Try a Hawaiian theme, which is easy in ideas, more work in preparation. Leis for all as they arrive at the party, and a paper flower to pin over an ear. Have pineapple upside down cake with papaya or guava juice. A big treat here are the Hula dancers from a local dancing school.

A circus theme, king for a day theme, a work day to help

someone else theme—these will occupy the elderly for some time, in planning.

A "just because" party can be the most rewarding. Base it on the first day up for someone who has been in bed for a long time, or the first time walking for someone who has been in a cast, or upon the return of a traveling member of the group. When the rain stops and the sun comes out, when the leaves start to turn color, or when the winter seems to be over—any one of these can be a basis for a "just because" party.

Be sure to have lots of volunteer helpers on hand for parties. Everyone wants to be served almost simultaneously, and it is at times such as this when tempers may rise. Try to be fair with all and keep a level head. If the party-goers know you are trying hard, they will be more patient and considerate. You set the tone and pace here by being considerate in the first place.

Good ideas will come in the mail if you subscribe to or ask for copies of newsletters from other institutions or agencies for the senior citizen. Be sure to read them throughly.

THE OPEN HOUSE

Changes, additions, and new services within a facility can be introduced to the community and those interested, by an Open House. Since this festivity is a form of public relations, it becomes important to plan well for smoothness of operation as well as to provide fun, information, and enjoyment for all.

Here again it is a good idea to list necessary ingredients, and those things which bring out the good points you have to offer. The features which you wish to tell the public about your facility may be its friendly atmosphere, good patient care, activities in which the elderly may participate, new facilities or services, additional space or any other features. Gear your celebration to what you want to get across. Plan new ways to do this. Be original.

In order to have a successful Open House, it is essential that long range plans, minute details, and foresight of what may happen are faced and solved well ahead of time. Usually the experience of conducting an Open House will provide the necessary background, but for those Activity Program Directors who are about to have their first one, the following are some ideas.

Don't tie yourself up in any one part of the celebration. Be a floater, free to help where needed by last minute changes and occurrences, to reassure, rearrange, and "make it go." Put into function your knowledge of the community, the individual people who have talents, the groups which offer an unusually attractive and enjoyable display of entertainment. Use your ability to organize and program the time allotted for the best use of these talents. Make it a pleasurable time for the entertainers, as well as the residents and visitors.

If you have a new dining room which will be featured, locate your most attractive event there—perhaps it is special music, an art show, the ever popular food, or a bazaar table.

If your facility caters to the retired and able senior citizen, the emphasis should be on the active things to do and plan for filling the waking hours of your residents.

Perhaps your Open House is to introduce a new wing for the confused and mentally dependent person, whose body is well but whose mind is not oriented to time, place, and awareness. Here the emphasis would be geared to motivation, remotivation, and activities to attract this individual to a more responsible life.

Are you offering a day care service? Show the public what will happen to their family member when they are left in your care for those three to twelve hour periods.

Again, make your plans according to what you have to tell. Scheduling of the time of year, day of week, and hour of the day for your Open House should be carefully considered. Perhaps the anniversary of the first opening, the dedication of the new building, or the formation of the group, is the basis for the decision. At any rate, Sunday afternoon seems to be universally popular, when people, both visitors and residents, are free of regular responsibilities, and are able to enjoy the entertainment, food, and sociability. The house should be spic and span, with flowers and other decorations to make it attractive.

Ingredients for Open House

1. Special Music and Entertainment. This feature, if well planned, will draw interested people from the community, and appeal to the elderly. Everyone loves peppy, well presented music and lively entertainment. Try using a local musical group, community or high school band, combo, hill billy group, or several wandering musical troubadours. Give some thought to a magician, a juggler, a balloon man (who makes animals from twisting long balloons). Each of these ideas requires planning for successful presentation. When you have a group such as a band, combo, or even a magician, chairs, space, lights and an attentive stationary audience are needed. Mobile, single performers are

easier to handle. They can wander about, wherever there is room and a group to enjoy it. A juggler or balloon man might need a mobile table from which to work.

Volunteer helpers who are familiar with your facility will be most useful. Assign one to each entertainer or group to be available as needed. Provide each hostess with a name badge, medallion, single flower, corsage, or some easily recognized identification, saying "Host" or "Hostess."

2. Tours. These are an essential ingredient for an Open House. Tours for your visitors are a means of seeing your facility and the reason for going to this effort. This is the area where staff members and persons *very* familiar with the facility are used as guides. They have to be able to answer questions and know the policies. Therefore, the average volunteers may not be adequate. There are always exceptions, but take care to have the tour guides well prepared for their fatiguing jobs. Have them identified as guides, and stationed at the main entrance, to be available to the interested visitors as they enter.

Perhaps you have prepared a slide show of your facility in everyday action and functions. This would be great for an Open House, provided you have the space to allot for darkening and continuous use for the two to three hour period.

Your scrap books should be in good order and prominently displayed for those who wish to see what has gone before. The guest book may be handled by a senior citizen at the main entrance. Choose one who likes people, knows the facility, and does not tire easily in a static job. Provide him or her with a comfortable chair and several pens.

3. Refreshments. The refreshments and food should be easily accessible, attractively laid and tastily prepared. The season of the year will play some part in what you serve, but coffee seems to be a basic. Try dispensers located in several convenient places. Disposable cups and napkins, cream, sugar, and a waste container will complete peoples' needs.

Simplicity in additional goodies should be the theme. Punch and cookies are good. The elderly may volunteer to make the cookies as a pre-Open House activity.

Place the table in an open area where you have ample room and people can come and go freely. Volunteer hostesses to set the table and serve the guests are most helpful. If you give them the responsibility of the whole job, they'll probably bring their own table cloth, flowers, aprons, and ideas. Encourage this since it again involves the public in the activities of the facility. However, the residents may wish to do all of the preparation and make all of the arrangements themselves, even to cooking and rolling popcorn balls during the Open House. This, too, should be encouraged if they are capable.

4. Art Shows and Displays from the Community. These types of exhibits involve outsiders. They are extra work for you, but do provide a refreshing addition to the facility. They bring friends to see the artists' work. Your resident senior citizens will be able to enjoy having a touch of modern living from the outside. This is a good public relations effort. Remember your efforts here are for the residents as much as for the guests. Provide security for these displays by stationing volunteer hosts and hostesses with the exhibit. Perhaps the artists will be happy to be present to explain and comment. These exhibits must be arranged for in advance and hung ahead of time. You will inevitably be responsible for the actual materials and equipment for hanging and displaying, such as: nails, hammer, tape, wire, string, signs, cardboard, pens, and scissors. Plan ahead and be ready.

5. Bazaar and Sales Table. Open House is a wonderful opportunity for display and sale of products made by the residents in the activity program throughout the year. Sales can be very successful and are usually tax free on the basis of an occasional sale. Locate the table in an open area for free circulation of customers, perhaps near the goodies. Make it attractive and not too crowded with items. Man it with enthusiastic senior citizens who have had a hand in making the products. One of them can be treasurer. Provide change and a box. Each item should be priced with a tag ahead of time. Volunteer hostesses can be used in this area if the elderly are not desirous or capable of taking the responsibility.

Prizes will enliven the festivities. Place a cross of colored tape on the floor near the bazaar table and set an alarm clock to go off during Open House hours. The person standing nearest the cross when the clock rings wins a previously selected prize. Guessing contests are also an intriguing addition. The preparation of beans or buttons in a jar will take some resident's effort and interest ahead of time to have an accurate figure upon which to award the prize. Papers, pencils, and a deposit box also are needed.

Funds from this sales table can be used to acquire additional tools and equipment for the activity program. Orders can be taken at this time for special items to be made up later on as time allows.

6. Publicity and Communications. Since the Activity Program Director's job includes contact with the community, the volunteers and the residents' families, she should be in charge of getting publicity underway.

If you want people to come to an Open House, you must let them know about it. Use any way you can to get the information across involving as many outsiders as possible in the function itself. Being on good terms with the local press, the neighborhood club newsletters and bulletins, the feature writers and editors of the daily papers, will all be helpful. If you buy an advertisement in the classified section of the paper, you'll usually get additional voluntary coverage devoted to your activity. Printed invitations and announcements, individually addressed and mailed, are a lot of work and expense, but pay off because of the personal touch. At least the individual knows about your efforts whether he is able to be present or not. Developing a mailing list will take a long time and much thought. Try to prepare it in a permanent fashion for use later on Christmas cards, departmental, and personnel announcements. The administrator and all department heads should contribute to this list. If your activity program is connected with an organization such as Y.W.C.A., church, or other established functioning group, there will be a ready mailing list from which to work.

Posters, placed on bulletin boards, in store windows, at the library, and community gathering spots, will attract some interest. Be sure this is the type of publicity you and the Administrator desire, before going to all of the work. It is a great deal of work to make and distribute posters of a size which are effective.

Signs made for use within the facility, to publicize the Open House to residents, visitors, families, and staff, are very useful. The basic "A" shaped sign, with a firm, wide base, and changeable fronts, is easiest to make and most stable. Not only are these useful for Open House, but can be used daily for announcements or communications.

If you publish a newsletter within the scope of your activity program, be sure to mention the Open House in it at least a month ahead. Extra copies of this can be mailed to a select group also. Be sure to put the newsletters in envelopes. Better care in handling will result.

The old time "sandwich man" sign board should be considered. Certain senior citizens get a chuckle out of being a part of such antics. If used sparingly, and within a limited gathering or specially interested group of people, it can attract attention. It should be carefully planned and skillfully used.

MAKING HOLIDAYS FESTIVE

Some months have more than their share of official holidays. February, the shortest month, has four well known ones: Ground Hog Day, Lincoln's and Washington's birthdays, and Valentine's Day. On the other hand, in August, there are no assigned holidays at all, but you can create a festive non-holiday especially for your residents. Pack it with lots of personal touches and kindnesses. One non-holiday might include "Flower Day," when each one has a fresh flower to wear, donated perhaps by a garden club. The supermarket may save their discarded advertising decorations for you and these will brighten a rainy day.

Simple, small things make an ordinary day something special, particularly for those whose days are all alike and routine. Use a small battery operated toy train, chugging and tooting its way around the halls, bright and early in the day, to limber up those smiles and recall earlier childhoods.

Suggest to the residents that they create costumes for prizes. Cartons, with shoulder straps, decorated and worn over regular clothing can be hilarious. Draw a picture of an old car on one and suggest to the wearer that he walk in the manner of an old car in motion. Animal designs can also be used. Let your ideas have full rein in this area, if you have the type of senior citizens who will go along with this kind of non-holiday festivity.

Style shows of various types can be very entertaining. Old fashioned clothing can be modeled by residents, for example, striped pants, swallow-tail coat, and top hat for the men. Also, a local dress shop may present a style show with your volunteers as models. This will create much interest among the residents and keep them up to date also. It involves the community in your program once again.

Most people think of holidays as those gay days when one sleeps late, has picnics, thinks of pleasures for himself and his family, and in general takes a day off. You, as an Activity Program Director must make these days extra special in some little way for your senior citizens who are unable to go out.

As an example, Fathers' Day always falls on Sunday, and in an institution some residents will have visitors, but some won't. All of them, men and women alike, will enjoy seeing some old time cars, like the ones in which they used to ride. Ask an antique car club or local member to bring over a couple of vintage cars. Once we had a Stanley Steamer which was painted red. The owner gave rides, explained the engine, and filled up his tank from our garden hose for his homeward trip. Our residents looked forward to that day, which was made a little bit different by a kindly person and his hobby.

Another time we invited the local fire department (we are located in a small surburban town) to bring an engine over and exercise our hydrants for the benefit of our residents. They loved it! And—the fire department discovered one hydrant which didn't function properly. So, it was a profitable arrangement all around.

You might reverse these two ideas by taking your senior citizens to an old car festival or to the fire station, depending upon their physical ability. That will make a day a little bit different also.

A few simple ingredients can make a plain day into a holiday, such as, decorations, special foods (or ways of serving them), music, costumes, unusual hats, fashion show, visitors, and individual gifts. One of the nicest things that happens at Issaquah Villa is the presenting of a fresh red rose to each resident on his birthday. Our Lady Lions Club has done this for many years. It certainly makes a festive occasion for the birthday person.

Plan decorations for each month. How about easily digested Chinese fortune cookies on New Year's Day, to prophesy the year to come? Gear your decorations to the main holiday of each month, with a party planned around that holiday. If you plan your own non-holiday party, put a twist into it. Be original in the favors, place mats, decorations, costumes, food, and entertainment.

Making all holidays, whether real or created, gay and enjoyable to the majority of your charges, is a matter of using imagination, ingenuity, and resourcefulness. When you find a resident, family member, friend, or volunteer who has an unusual talent, make use of it in some way. Plan a party around it. In this way, you can continually add spirit to the routine lives of your senior citizens.

FUN AND GAMES—ACTIVE

It takes a person with special interests and abilities to lead active games. It also takes adapted equipment, space and techniques of motivation to encourage the elderly to participate in this kind of physical activity. If the residents are allowed to arrange their own games voluntarily, they are very likely never to get around to it so a leader is necessary. This person must be an active organizer; one who has the enthusiasm and energy to pick up the tempo when it lags. Whether she or he is a volunteer, a staff member or a resident makes no difference as long as he is there to start things off and keep the spark. By keeping the spark we mean: being able to find and express accomplishment for the losers as well as the winners; being able to switch methods and techniques of playing games as needed; being able to adapt the game psychologically for encouragement and satisfaction; and being able to maintain a lighthearted attitude of enjoyment for all, rather than a serious "I have to win" attitude on the part of the participants. If the first introductions to these recreational experiences have been successful, the more able participants will carry on eagerly, pretty much on their own when it is necessary.

Good sources of help in this area come from people in the recreation field, (park departments, Y.M.C.A.), from books in the library and from the senior citizens themselves. The many collections and lists of active games in books, circulars and pamphlets can be helpful if the Activity Program Director will adapt them for the physical limitations and the needs of her particular senior citizens.

New and different ideas are hard to introduce and will take much time in physical and psychological preparation and activation before the equipment, leaders and residents are all ready. This is the point at which the spark of enthusiasm has to be ignited or the project will not be successful. Do not give up or be discouraged because of suspicious or hostile attitudes toward your ideas. Older people like to be coaxed, in a firm but friendly way.

Pick out a senior citizen who has the respect of his peers, who is able to convince others and hold their admiration. Begin your first efforts here. If you can encourage him to do some of the planning and organizing, half your battle is won. This will take time. Three to six months is an average time in which to tailor all the needs and equipment for success, to the individuals who will participate. Remember, they work, act and learn at a less rapid pace than twenty to thirty year olds. Besides they have physical, emotional, and social limitations to be considered. The flip of the wrist and the muscle power to throw darts reacts more like coldflowing molasses at this age.

For instance, in laying out an area for shuffleboard, the court can be shortened, and perhaps even the handles of the cues will have to be adjusted, especially if wheel chair occupants are involved. Adjustments are needed in active games according to the ability level, energy output and physical capacity of the participants. The time for scheduling this type of activity should be in the morning or early afternoon when energy levels are high. The leader must be aware of these limitations and base active games on institutional and individual need.

Exercise and play in recreation is as respectable a pastime as is work and material accomplishment. It is a way to make new friends and to learn new things about old friends. It contributes to the physical well-being, keeps the body in tone, and adds a zest to living. The competitive aspect of playing games has plus and minus values for older people. The Activity Program Director must be sure competition is kept on a friendly basis, with no partiality shown.

The following active games, when modified to meet the needs of the group, will be enjoyable and provide maximum personal participation:

Bowling (plastic pins and rubber ball)
Bean bag throwing (shorten distance)

Golfing, (use of an indoor "Putnik")
Shuffleboard
Darts
Rubber quoits
Ring toss
Basketball and football throw
Circle games (sit down to play)
Relay games (sit down to play)

FUN AND GAMES–SEDENTARY

Someone has defined time as "the measure of things that change." One of the responsibilities of an Activity Program Director is to be sure that time holds changes for those who are unable to make things change for themselves. This especially refers to those who are sedentary and housebound. They will appreciate your efforts to bring activities, ideas and new experiences to them. Since older people like a schedule of regular daily routine, some of the following suggestions should be arranged on this basis and have firm commitment without fail.

Afternoon tea is one of these regular commitments. Juice, coffee and tea, with crackers, served from a cart pushed through the halls and into the dining room can become a regularly anticipated social period for those confined to indoors. It affords the opportunity for families and friends to visit and have something to do while chatting.

Also at tea time, announcements can be made, contests or displays held to arouse interest. The residents will start saying, "What will be going on this afternoon? Guess I better go and see." Encourage them to play the piano and sing. Offer a prize for the person guessing the number of buttons in a jar, or putting the last piece in a jigsaw puzzle.

Once a month at tea time have an educational exhibit. The senior citizens enjoy reminders of their early lives such as dolls, toys, buttons, or the spinning of wool. And they will love to tell you all about the things they had and what happened to them. You draw them into the activities in this way. The Activity Program Director should make it a point each day at tea time to circulate among the residents and their guests, showing interest in what is going on and who is there. They will appreciate your interest and perhaps you can be of help also. In this way much is learned about residents and their families.

Start each day with a weather report, the one the weatherman has predicted. It might be announced over the intercom or printed on slips of paper at the breakfast table. After a few days of straight forward reports when you know there has been aroused an interest, throw in a couple of laughs to start the day off happy. Use comments from Mark Twain, "Nobody does anything about the weather", or from *Winnie The Pooh,* "We haven't had an earthquake lately." There will be reactions from the alert people and soon one will be helping with the project.

Types of quiet and skill games for 2 to 4 people are endless. Card games, (with large print), checkers, chess, anagrams, dominoes, cribbage, jigsaw puzzles and many modifications are available. Your public library has many books on these subjects. Games and contests should stimulate general interest and awareness in the program. Be sure the games are adapted for and geared to adults. If they have a skill connected with them, so much the better.

Senior citizens will love to play bingo, if you can convince them that they are able to and if you make arrangements which do not smack of gambling. Do not charge for playing. Have no money connected with the operation in any way. Many older people have strong feelings about this aspect of bingo. Provide prizes, gift-wrapped by volunteers and separated into boxes marked "Men" and "Ladies." For prizes use white elephants, samples, castoffs in good condition, ceramic knickknacks, fruit, window plants, and even childrens' small toys. The winners can use these as gifts for family and friends. With proper promotion, families, friends and volunteers will provide a good number of prizes free of charge. You may even locate the excess and leftovers from a gift shop in this way.

Modification of the usual bingo equipment will encourage those with poor hearing, eyesight and manual dexterity. Pips for covering the numbers can be made from ½" or 3/8" doweling, cut ¼" thick. Buttons also are easy for old stiff fingers to pick up. The cards can be held in place with loops of sticky tape. For those who are hard of hearing, the numbers may be written on a blackboard as they are called. The usual straight line bingo rules may be varied. For example, the first person to cover all four corners can be declared the winner. The use of proper names written on blank cards in place of numbers can be an interesting innovation.

Other sedentary fun for groups can consist of:

Films and slides. Available from libraries, airlines, oil companies, consulates, families, friends and volunteers.

Discussion groups. Stimulate with use of items or pictures.

Singing sessions. Use familiar music and large print word sheets.

Invite a local artist to come to tea and sketch a couple of the senior citizens. This is very successful, especially if you select those who need a lift. The Fuller Brush man and the Avon lady will love to come and show their products. This is a wonderful way to create discussion about new products and new ways of doing old familiar tasks.

Contests as entertainment are a challenge. Age guessing is always popular with the geriatrics crowd. They are proud to be 90 years old and still going strong. "When is your birthday? And, how old will you be? I'll be 93 in October." This type of conversation goes on and on.

Almost all senior citizens develop an interest in some form of religious contact. They derive much pleasure and enjoyment from a weekly period of devotion. If you have no chapel available, use the dining room, social or day room by moving the chairs around and constructing a portable altar and lectern. Each denomination can then select its need. A piano or organ is useful but someone playing the guitar or accordian will be as effective. Regularly scheduled services can be arranged with your local ministerial association, alternating denominations and ministers. At Issaquah Villa we have chosen Friday morning for our weekly church service. Six denominations participate, make their own schedule, use our large print hymn books and at times ask one of our residents to accompany the singing. Two volunteers come each week to help the elderly to and from the service.

If you are fortunate enough to have some musicians among your residents be sure to use them at every opportunity. It will bring them out of their rooms, their loneliness and doldrums, and stimulate them to want to be a part of what is going on.

Section III

CREATIVE HANDICRAFT
PROJECTS

Chapter 10

GUIDELINES FOR
POSITIVE RESULTS

Time is the most common ingredient available when you are a senior citizen, but it seems to disappear faster than ever. Why? Because, as you get older, tasks take longer and require more energy to accomplish. Lifetime skills are usually slowing, reaction time is lengthening, manual dexterity is stiffening, eyesight is becoming blurred, mental attitudes are static and regressing, especially if the physical condition is not up to par. These deteriorating factors are not necessarily all present in all types of people at any specific time or age. However, all of us are aware of the slowing process beginning at about 50-55 years of age. So, it is a good thing that time is available when it takes longer to accomplish our daily routines.

For those of us who work with these senior citizens, it is a constant challenge to be able to adapt, adjust, and rearrange activities and projects so that enjoyment is evident and progress is made with a minimum of help, pushing and fussing. Mental confusion can result from using too much of the last two techniques.

In this project section, we will attempt to present ideas which can be expanded, adapted, and developed according to the need of the program and the individual patient.

Certain assumptions are made. We assume the Activity Program Director has some basic knowledge of handicraft skills and techniques, that she has had at least the equivalent of a high school home economics sewing course, and had experimented with various craft mediums. These would include: waste materials, wood, simple clays and ceramics, knitting, crocheting, papers, paints, glues, etc. She should also have some personal talents and interests which will be useful in developing the additional necessary program. These might include: tumbling rocks, spinning wool, painting by number, photography, etc. It cannot be overemphasized that the Activity Program Director should be constantly and enthusiastically searching for new techniques, new materials, new products, and new combinations of both the new and old.

The following is a list of general principles to be used in planning projects for senior citizens, keeping in mind that the elderly have had many learning experiences, which although slowing now, are nevertheless very real to them.

1. *Keep everything simple and easy to enjoy.* Present one thing at a time, one step at a time on a project, and not too many things to watch or think about at a given moment. Make design easy to cut, color, paste, sew, handle and understand.

2. *Keep everything natural, real, and genuine.* In designs for dolls and stuffed toys, use only those which look like the item they represent, legs where they should be, features normal, etc. Avoid exaggerated and grotesque designs. They are confusing to the older person. Extremely small arms and legs and long, narrow necks are difficult for old, stiff fingers to turn, stuff, and assemble.

3. *Keep everything functional, useful, and practical.* Be sure there is a reason and use for what is made. Don't have a resident make something useless: make it for someone and some use. Practicality pays off in several areas, such as: making commercial patterns useful and durable over a long period by pasting them onto butcher paper first, using good design, materials, color and workmanship, using paints and materials which will easily be removed from hands, and protecting clothing from permanent damage.

4. *Use light and bright colors in all handwork and crafts.* Old eyes do not distinguish between dark colors and shades. Contrasts within light colors, tints and an accent shade can be successful, but in the main stick to gay, bright colors in cloth, yarn, paint, weaving, etc.

5. *Use contrasts in signs and attention getting features.* For example, a sign on a bulletin board to call attention to a special entertainment, should be made to catch the eye in line, color, or design. Try adapting a battery operated unit donated from the supermarket. It will have motion and attract attention.

6. *Use firm but soft textures in materials.* Old skin is tender and reacts to harsh and coarse surfaces. You might lose an elderly person's interest in this manner right in the very beginning. Older people depend upon their feeling ability to help out failing eyesight. Confusion and messiness distracts the elderly, and, extremely irregular textures can contribute to this problem.

7. *Be sure the activity is meaningful to the resident.* Each senior citizen needs individual attention, a goal at his level of ability, and enjoyment in reaching that goal. Sometimes it is mutually beneficial if two people help each other.

8. *Break down patterns and projects into their simplest form.* Here is the basic doll pattern simplified:
   1. Head and body
   2. Arms, identical and interchangeable.
   3. Legs, identical and interchangeable.

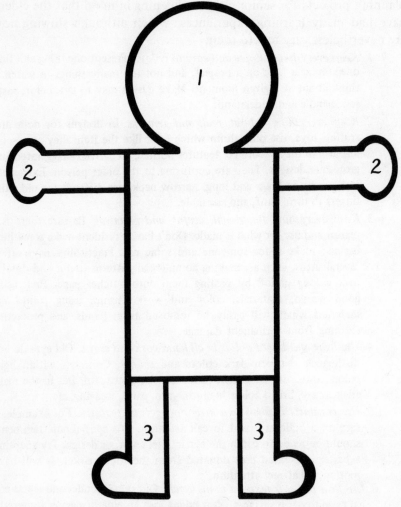

Figure 10-1

This pattern could be used in one piece, but if you cut the arms and legs from the body, there is more economical use of fabric. It is easier to stuff, and the elderly will understand its assembly better. Follow this system in all projects.

9. *Give simple instructions, one step at a time.* Be familiar with the project and explain only one step at a time. Have a sample of the finished product to help with questions. Give directions in few words and only when a point of need has been reached. Some of your charges can forge ahead with simple guidance in good design, color and texture. If you have made the item yourself, you will know how to plan and prepare it, possible difficulties to anticipate, how and when to inspire and encourage extra effort.

10. *Be willing and able to change your instruction form when necessary.* If your instructions are not understood, one of several things is at fault: the project is too advanced, the instructions are too complicated, or some distraction has occurred. Try a second time with simpler words, and do not show irritation. If this doesn't work, change the subject, ask a question and direct the subject to the resident himself. You'll soon learn the problem. Most workers like their projects all laid out for them and a regular spot in the room which is theirs. This tells them they are wanted.

11. *Be willing to assume responsibility for any unfortunate results.* Take all of the blame on yourself. Also be able to capitalize on mistakes. As an example: A head is stitched on an animal crooked. Change the facial expression to one which fits the posture. Have alternate paths to follow in case of error.

12. *Accept and use the senior citizen's ideas and suggestions.* This is an excellent way to gain confidence. Many of their ideas are great, but will need adaptation. When used, give credit where credit is due.

13. *Purchase durable supplies and equipment.* You get what you pay for in every sense. If you want a quality activity, start with quality ingredients kept in good condition.

14. *Provide a hard surface for work.* Sometimes a light background under the work will help old eyes see the work.

15. *Avoid small scale activities.* Keep things large, familiar, and audible. Avoid having a resident say, "I used to be able to do it, and it makes me mad now that I can't." Here is where frustration starts. Use large, plain masses in design.

16. *Keep techniques familiar.* Encourage the person to stick to things he can do well in his own way. Use familiar techniques in new ways, such as weaving with ribbons instead of thread.

While making plans for an individual project, have a direction in mind for its use. Perhaps the resident has a favorite grandchild, family member, or friend who may be the recipient. He may make a second similar item for the disposal of the department. Thus, the first one for the senior citizen and the second one for the shop becomes a workable arrangement. In this way income from projects pays for new materials. If some of the items do not sell, try putting a bag together for a children's hospital or pre-school, the ship HOPE, or Dr. Pat Smith's hospital in Vietnam. Identify them with a tag for the good public relations and new resulting friendships.

Prices of items can be based on material cost plus 20 percent to 30 percent. If good donated materials are used, relate the cost to that of purchased ones. Sales outlets may be located in the facility workshop or in a nearby community gift shop. In the latter arrangement, it would be a good idea to arrange for the person making the product to receive the amount above the cost of materials for his own profit. In this way quality control can be exerted in the items to be placed for outside sale.

As Activity Program Director, think in terms of the people with whom you are working. Put yourself in their shoes and then design for them.

Chapter 11

HOW TO MAKE
STUFFED ANIMALS

The exact therapeutic value of creating a 10 inch high stuffed purple cow has probably never been measured, but quite a few groups of elderly patients have spent many pleasant hours on just such a project. It isn't necessary, or even desirable, to specialize in off-color farm stock; any kind of stuffed animal toy provides an excellent outlet for the talent of convalescing residents.

That's the nice thing about this particular breed of project; the possibilities for variety are nearly endless. Not only can a wide range of patterns be matched to available skill (both yours and the patients'), but even common animals such as cats and dogs can be made individually appealing by simple imaginative twists. Turn a head sideways, for instance, add a hat with a feather in it, or put a flower in a paw. Change the angle of the whiskers, add boots and gloves, or use spotted or striped cloth instead of plain colors. Remember, however, that older people usually want realism in the things they make, and, while a giraffe or tiger might occasionally be a great success in a wild, all-over print, your animals should usually be representative of their kind.

Stuffed animals are not a one-person or one-day project. Several people will be involved for a considerable period of time, sometimes two or three days, sometimes several weeks. You can thus distribute various parts of the work to patients who have different degrees of ability and keep each of the members of a sizable group occupied at his best working level.

Properly made stuffed toys are readily saleable if your institution permits such commercialism. If you cannot sell them, patients, visitors and staff will use all you can make as presents for their children and grandchildren. In any case, your patients will get particular satisfaction from making stuffed animals because of the pleasure which other people derive from use of these products.

A variety of materials may be used for animal stuffing. The two kinds found to be most suitable are cut up nylon stockings (if the cover material doesn't let the dark color show through), and strips of white artificial fiber material used for ski jacket insulation. A huge supply of nylons can be obtained from a collection drive at any junior or senior high school; the jacket material you get by persuading a manufacturer to save his cutting scraps for you. Both kinds of material may be packed either loosely or tightly as required by the animal's character and configuration, and both will dry quickly when the toy is dropped in the bathtub by a careless young owner.

Shredded foam rubber scraps, cotton or artificial fiber batting, or Kapok can also be used for animal filling if you find them easier to obtain. These materials, however, do not dry readily and will eventually become lumpy inside the toy.

Stuffing is pushed into legs, arms, tails and other small places with a piece of 3/16" or ¼" dowelling, 12" long, which has been tapered on one end. A pencil sharpener will form the taper if you are careful not to make too sharp a point. Pad the other end with a wad of cotton wrapped in masking tape, to protect the hand of the worker.

PATTERNS AND DIRECTIONS

The following five representative examples of stuffed animal projects are arranged in order of increasing complexity to help you select the level which is best for a given application. If you are not sure what your patients can do, start at the beginning and work up; the directions will tell you the principal things to look for as you make each progression.

BABY LION

(First Level of Complexity)

This is the simplest kind of pattern, typical of ones which you can make from pictures in childrens' coloring books.

1. Cut identical front and back pieces, adding 3/8" seam allowance to original size of picture.
2. Stitch the two pieces together, with right sides of material facing each other. Leave an opening as indicated, for putting in the stuffing.
3. Turn the stitched body right side out.
4. Stuff.
5. Apply face. Use paint, felt pen, sewn-on felt, or even embroidery if someone wants to take the time.
6. For extra effect add a mane or ruff of fringe encircling the head, and a tassel of wool on the tip of the tail.

BABY LION

CUT TWO

Leave open

Figure 11-1

An item such as the PANDA BEAR can be made in the same first-level way as the lion, but given variety by sewing on an additional set of front and back leg pieces cut from striped or print material. Black ears, eyes, nose and paws are put on with a felt pen. To make a two-legged animal like the panda stand up, sew an empty thread spool, with its axis horizontal (on its side), to the bottom of each foot.

KITTEN

(Second Level of Complexity)

Some additional operations are required to build two or more kinds of materials into an animal. Application of the ears to this kitten illustrates the procedure. The whole animal is made as follows:

1. Cut identical front and back body pieces.
2. Cut four ear pieces. Use two contrasting colors of material.
3. Stitch the pairs of ear pieces together, two colors in each pair, then turn ears right side out. If you want stuffed, stand-up ears, put the stuffing in now, otherwise they'll go on limp. Either way is all right, depending on what effect you want.
4. Pin the ears in place on one of the body pieces. Be sure to place them upside down, with the points down, so that they will come out right side up when the body is turned inside out after stitching. Also be sure

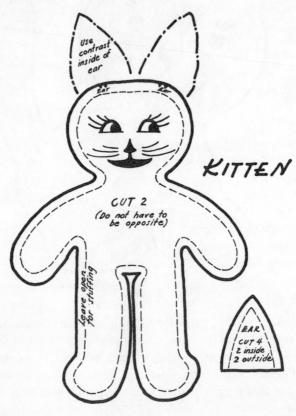

Figure 11-2

that right sides of ear and body materials are together, for the same reason.

5. Stitch the two body pieces together, with the ears inside between them. Leave the stuffing slit open.

6. Turn body right side out.

7. Stuff.

8. Apply face.

DUCK

(Third Level of Complexity)

This four-piece design illustrates another way to combine multiple materials. Here a definite three-dimensional effect is obtained by assembling the component parts after stitching, stuffing and turning each one inside-out. A project of this level can be divided among at least four people. The steps are: (Figure 11-3)

1. Draw patterns on cloth. (Warn whoever does this about the unsymmetrical head, it must be reversed each time.) Use yellow felt for body and head, orange felt for beak and tail. Other materials, such as deep pile fabric or regular firm cotton may also be used, of course, as long as the color and texture are reasonably realistic.

2. Cut out pieces. Don't forget the neck slot in the top body piece.

3. Pin tail and beak in place on body and neck pieces. Point them to the inside so that they will be heading the right way when the body and neck are turned after stitching.

4. Pin body and head pieces for stitching.

5. Stitch body and head; two separate assemblies.

6. Turn body and head right side out. (Be careful who gets this job, it can be frustrating for old fingers. You or a strong-handed helper may have to assist.)

7. Stuff body and head.

8. Hand-stitch head to body.

9. Apply button eyes and neck ribbon.

When your group begins to tire of duck production, show them how to make turtles from the same pattern by leaving off the beak, adding four feet, and substituting a pointed tail. Complete the metamorphosis by shortening and changing the angle of the neck.

PIG

(Fourth Level of Complexity)

This project introduces more new features, such as a folded

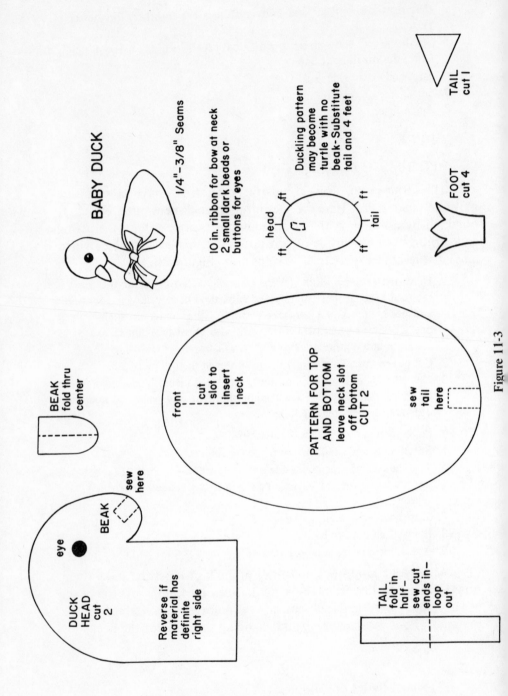

BABY DUCK

1/4"–3/8" Seams

10 in. ribbon for bow at neck
2 small dark beads or
buttons for eyes

Duckling pattern
may become
turtle with no
beak–Substitute
tail and 4 feet

head
ft
ft
ft
ft
tail

TAIL
cut 1

FOOT
cut 4

BEAK
fold thru
center

front
cut
slot to
insert
neck

PATTERN FOR TOP
AND BOTTOM
leave neck slot
off bottom
CUT 2

sew
tail
here

sew
here

eye
BEAK

DUCK
HEAD
cut
2

Reverse if
material has
definite
right side

TAIL
fold in
half –
sew cut
ends in–
loop
out

Figure 11-3

124

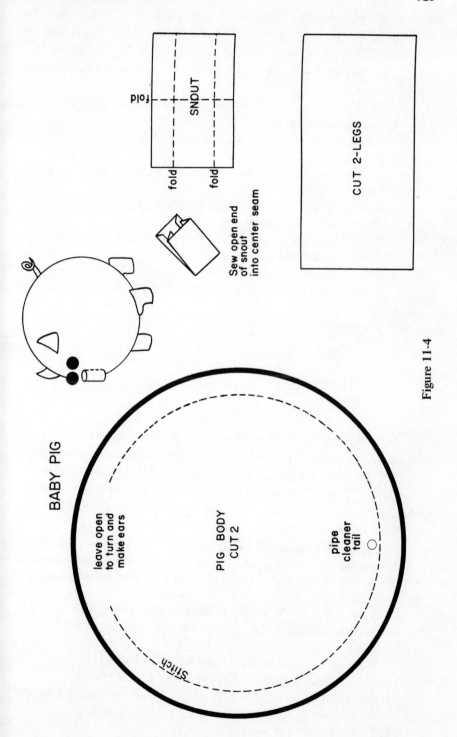

BABY PIG

SNOUT

fold

fold

fold

Sew open end
of snout
into center seam

CUT 2-LEGS

leave open
to turn and
make ears

PIG BODY
CUT 2

pipe
cleaner
tail

Stitch

Figure 11-4

cloth nose, pull-out ears, and use of pipe cleaners to stiffen legs. As with the duck, at least four people can be involved in the various operations. (Figure 11-4)

1. Cut two 6½" diameter circles of terry cloth or other rough textured material.
2. Stitch the circles together, leaving a 2" unsewn space.
3. Turn right side out, insert stuffing.
4. Cut two leg strips. Cut two pipe cleaners 5" long.
5. Roll each leg strip around one of the pipe cleaners, turn in the raw edges and whipstitch. Bend each rolled strip to fit the body and to leave two 1½" legs.
6. Sew legs firmly to front and rear underside of the body, on the side opposite the 2" open space.
7. Cut one rectangle for the snout. Fold on dotted lines, lengthwise first, then across the short way. Hand-stitch in place.
8. Form the ears from the unsewn part of the body circles by pulling excess cloth taut from the front. Stitch the ears together at the open side.
9. Make the tail from a single pipe cleaner twisted around a pencil. Sew in place.
10. Apply sequin or bead eyes.

RABBIT

(Fifth Level of Complexity)

Assembly of the 11 pieces in this pattern requires some sewing skill as well as ability to follow an extended sequence of operations. Much of the work on projects of this level will, therefore, have to be done by the younger, more alert patients or by a capable volunteer. Older patients can pin patterns, cut out the pieces, and stuff the assembled bodies and heads. (Figure 11-5 A, B, C)

1. Cut pieces as indicated on the pattern. Rabbits can be made of any durable, fuzzy material, and will be especially appealing if the inside of the ears and the top of the head are of a different color than the rest of the body.
2. Stitch edges of the six V's in the two back pieces. The tucks thus formed make the rabbit sit down (#1) and turn up his feet (#2 and #3).
3. Stitch the two back pieces together from crotch to neck.
4. Stitch the two front pieces together from crotch to neck.
5. Pin and stitch back to front, leaving a 2" or 3" opening for attaching the head later.
6. Turn body right side out.

7. Stitch pairs of ear pieces together, leaving the bottoms open.

8. Turn ears right side out, fold along line indicated, and stitch the fold. If you want the ears to stick straight up, sew in some stiffening material when you stitch the fold; otherwise the ears will flop out sideways. Try making them both ways to see which you like the best.

9. Pin and stitch ears to sides of the head, pointing down so that they will come out right when the head is turned right side out, and with the folded-in side toward the nose.

10. Pin head gusset to head pieces and stitch from nose to back of neck on both sides.

11. Stitch head pieces together at front and rear, from end of gusset down to the neck.

12. Turn head right side out.

13. Pin and stitch head to body, matching nose seam of head to front seam of body. Leave 2" to 3" opening at back of neck for inserting stuffing.

14. Stuff head and body.

15. Make and apply a pom-pom tail. (Pom-pom directions are in another chapter)

16. Make and apply felt eyes and nose, and wool whiskers.

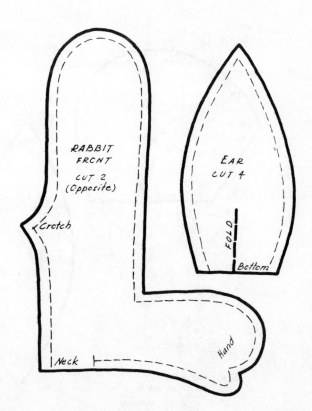

RABBIT
FRONT
CUT 2
(Opposite)

Crotch

Neck

EAR
CUT 4

FOLD

Bottom

Hand

Figure 11-5A

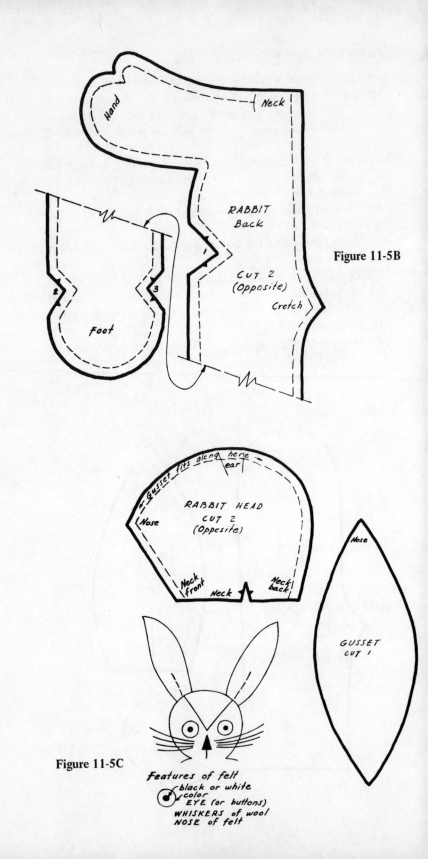

Hand

Neck

RABBIT
Back

CUT 2
(Opposite)

Crotch

Figure 11-5B

2

3

Foot

Gusset fits along here

ear

RABBIT HEAD
CUT 2
(Opposite)

Nose

Neck
front

Neck

Neck
back

Nose

GUSSET
CUT 1

Figure 11-5C

Features of felt
black or white
color
EYE (or buttons)
WHISKERS of wool
NOSE of felt

OTHER DESIGNS

Commercial patterns such as Simplicity or McCall's, or those published in women's magazines and the newspapers, are available in many sizes and all levels of complexity. You can easily collect a file of these which will include all of the standard animals as well as the more whimsical ones like the Winnie The Pooh series, then you can do some imaginative cross-breeding to develop your own designs. The "Tigger" of the Pooh series, for example, mutates into a really believable lion if you omit his stripes, add a mane, and put a tassel on the end of his tail.

Another source of patterns: used animal toys, either purchased or donated, ripped up and copied full scale. After you've done this a few times you will be able to design your own creations such as the Siamese cat and the white kitten. (Figure 11-6, 7)

Figure 11-6

Figure 11-7

Not all of the used items should be ripped up for patterns, however. Some of them make interesting renovation projects. A pink elephant, for instance, can be dyed dark blue, after unstuffing and washing him, then decorated with red, white and blue spots, fur eyebrows and bead eyes. Patriotic instead of pink, this animal can then serve his country by standing on the front desk with a donkey (of equal size) each election day to remind residents and guests of their voting duty.

A final word about stuffed animals. Whatever your source of designs, copied or renovated, add something distinctive of your own to each one. Make each creation a little bit special, a little bit more appealing than you found it. These stuffed toys aren't made to be hidden away in a closet, they are for pleasure to maker and user—pleasure in the creation and use of something different and a little bit personal.

Chapter 12

CREATING
BEAUTIFUL DOLLS

As people grow older, it is obvious how much they enjoy reminiscing about their younger years. They find great pleasure in little people, whether related to them or not. So it is understandable that they would be interested in making dolls. The pride in the completion of something useful is always a morale booster.

There are many good commercial patterns for dolls with easy to follow instructions. Use them whenever possible. You may find that you will be making several dozen of one style, if the results are attractive and pleasing. If you take orders, be sure there is no hurry on a completion date. All manner of interruptions can occur to interfere. Some residents will benefit from being pushed a little and encouraged to be a bit more diligent, but in the main, let them work at their own pace, when they want to, within reasonable hours of your schedule, and for as long as they desire at a time.

Be sure the patterns and directions are given in their simplest form. Do not choose too small a doll. Even a 10" doll becomes tedious to assemble, stuff and dress. The 15"-20" size is ideal, if you are working from scratch.

When making your own pattern, cut from sandpaper and use sand side down, thus eliminating pins. Or use old x-ray film, draw the outline and cut out.

If you have senior citizens with good manual dexterity, dolls can be made from spools, beads and corks. They may be wired together to be moveable, or glued together to stand stiffly. Details done with pipecleaners, paint, sequins and buttons add humor and appeal.

SKEIN DOLL

Materials: Pink or peach 4 ply yarn for body
Yellow or brown 4 ply yarn for hair.
Contrasting yarn to tie arms and legs.
1 piece of corrugated cardboard 4" x 8".
Wad of cotton or 1" styrofoam ball for head.

Directions: Wind body yarn around 8" side of cardboard 40 times.
At one end, tie tightly all 40 loops for top of head.
At opposite end tie 2 sets of 20 loops for feet.

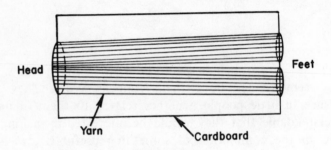

Head   **Feet**

Yarn   Cardboard

Figure 12-1

Slip a piece of paper between the two layers of the skein to keep them separated, and slide skein off cardboard.
Wind body yarn around 4" side of cardboard 20 times, for arms.
Tie tightly at each end of loops and slide off cardboard.

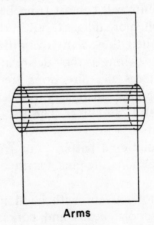

Arms

Figure 12-2

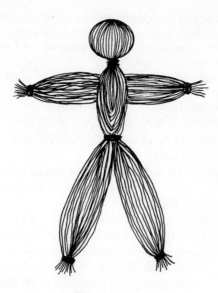

Figure 12-3

Figure 12-4

At top of body skein, insert head shaping material, distributing
yarn evenly around head to cover, at the same time
maintaining the separation of the two sides of the skein.

Tie tightly at neck.

Place the arm skein through the division, allowing it to
protrude evenly on each side for arms.

Tie tightly below arms for waist.

Tie ends of arms and legs, clip loops if desired. (Figure 12-3)

For wig: Braid loosely 12 strands of yarn 10" long.

Tie each end of the braid.

Spread the center of the braid and tack with thread and needle
across the top of the head from center forehead to nape
of neck.

Bangs may be sewn on with thread and needle.

A face may be embroidered or cut from felt and sewn on.

Character can be created by felt clothes, overalls, a flower in
the hand, buttons down the front, or make body of
colored yarn for Christmas or Halloween. (Figure 12-4)

RAGGEDY ANN AND ANDY

This is a complex, long term project which can involve several
people doing different parts but all working toward the same goal.
Capable workers can go along with only periodic supervision from
the Activity Program Director. She must be sure that arms look like
arms, feet face the same way and facial features are in correct
locations.

Materials: Use commercial pattern*.

Appropriate cloth for body and clothes.

Embroidery floss for face and heart.

Stuffing material.

Shoe buttons for eyes.

Sewing machine stitching is desirable for body.

Directions: Good ones come with the pattern.

Do body first. One person can cut, another assemble and pin
and a third can stitch.

Draw on and embroider face and heart before stitching body
together.

Stuff the body parts. This may be done by a rather limited
individual, and may take several days. (Make a stick
from doweling with the hand end padded for help in
stuffing the parts firmly and evenly.)

Hand sew the parts together, being sure of alignment.

*McCall Pattern, available at pattern counters.

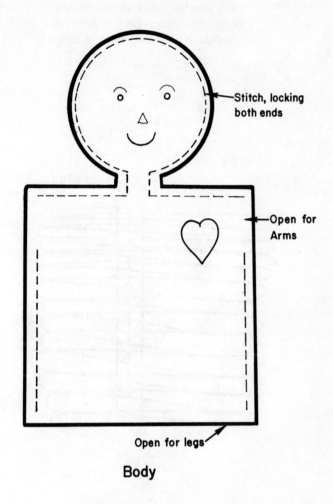

Body

Figure 12-5

Wig: Knitted. Using 4 ply red yarn and #8 needles, cast on 39
stitches. Knit one row. Second row, knit one stitch, yarn
over three times, knit one stitch, yarn over three times,
etc., to end of row (this make hair loops). Third row
knit. Repeat yarn over row and knit row until work
measures 4" ending with a knit row. Cast off. To
assemble, fold work with crease the narrow way of the
hair, sew together the cast off edge only. This will form
a cap. Tack it in place on head with loops outside.

Wig: Sewn. Use red yarn. Measure across top of head from
neck to neck. Cut a piece of twill tape this length. Using

small stitches, machine stitch yarn to this tape as is shown in diagram. Lock at both ends. Stitch yarn close together so tape does not show through.

Wig

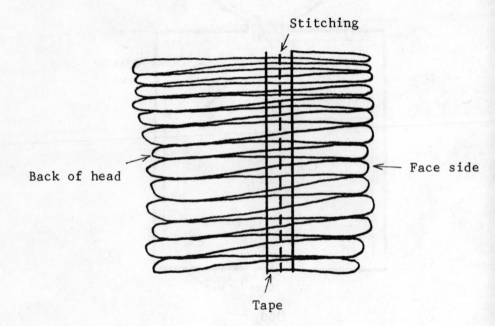

Stitching

Back of head

Face side

Tape

Figure 12-6

Sew tape across top of head from neck to neck, short loops forward, long ones back. Pass a piece of yarn through the back loops in consecutive order from one end to the other and fasten to the nape of the neck.

At the same time the body is being constructed, another group can be making the clothing. Here again the Activity Program Director will want to supervise assembly in order to assure success.

The same style of doll can be made into clowns and character dolls by a change of clothing and details.

Figure 12-7. Raggedy Ann.

Figure 12-8. Clown.

You may be given a child's baby doll or larger one to dress and renew. This is a great group project and involves more than the senior citizens. The giver will be interested in the result which provides good public relations. The facility's hairdresser will be happy to style the doll's wig. Donated cloth and trims will make wonderful clothes. Knitters can make sweaters and booties. Purses, necklaces, shoes, buntings, formals are some of the endless possibilities. Commercial doll clothes patterns are sold by the size of the doll. This project can take weeks and absorb many workers. It can make a good Christmas gift if you start soon enough.

Chapter 13

HOW TO CONSTRUCT
POM-POM ANIMALS

A simple project, one which can be used as a first step in getting an elderly person back to activity while still in bed. It not only exercises the fingers and arms, but it stimulates the mind to think ahead. It is a repetitive project for those with fair manual dexterity and limited eyesight.

Materials: Cardboard.
Yarn, scraps may be used.
Bits of felt for features.
Yarn needle.
Scissors.
Buttons for eyes.

Directions for one Pom-Pom:
Cut cardboard into appropriate size rings, with hole in center.
Use 2 cardboards for each one. The larger the circle, the larger the resulting pom-pom.

Figure 13-1

Wind yarn through hole and to outside around both rings. Continue until center hole is full. (When adding a piece of yarn, overlap or tie ends together, if dexterity is poor. Knots will be cut out when finishing.)

A yarn needle may be used at end to fill hole.

Cut yarn at outside of ring and between the two cardboards.

Figure 13-2

Tie, with a long piece of yarn between the two cardboard circles, pulling tightly and securing with a knot in the center of the rings. Leave ends long to use in fastening balls together.

Cut or tear each cardboard piece apart and remove.

Fluff ball to roundness, trim if necessary.

In assembling pom-pom animals, all threads must pass through the center of the ball. Details may be sewed on or glued with Barge Cement, available at shoe repair stores.

Mouse: (1) Make 1 gray wool ball.

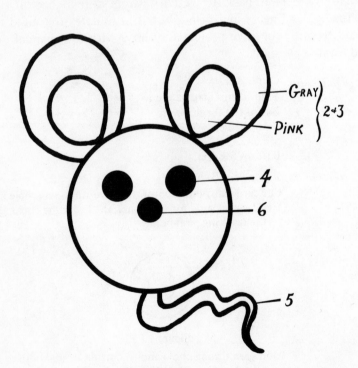

Figure 13-3

(2) Cut 2 ears of felt, gray outside and pink inside. Glue or tack together. The larger, the more effective the mouse.
(3) Tack the base of the ear together, and sew in place.
(4) Sew in place for eyes, two shiny black shoe buttons or beads.
(5) Cut a long curvy tail and tack in place.
(6) Round felt nose, put in place last.

Figure 13-4

Zonk: (1) Make 1 wool ball, any size, any color (this pattern is 3" ball).
(2) Cut feet of felt.
(3) Cut nose of felt.
(4) Use buttons or commercial eyes.
(5) Feathers for tail.

Figure 13-5

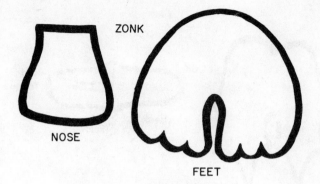

ZONK

NOSE

FEET

Figure 13-6

Duck: (1) Make 2 yellow pom-poms, one may be larger.
           (2) Tie balls together.
           (3) Cut from felt, orange beak and feet.
           (4) Red tongue may be glued inside beak.
           (5) Sew together in place: feet, beak, and eyes.

DUCK

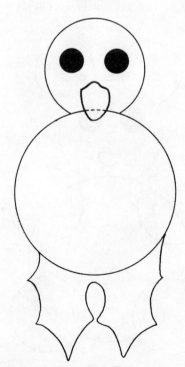

Figure 13-7

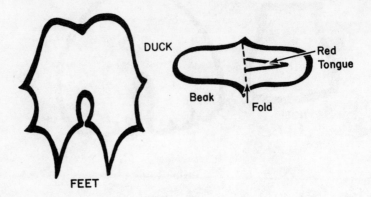

Figure 13-8

Bear: (1) Make 2 large and 5 small pom-poms.

           (2) Tie the larger ones together for body and head.

           (3) Sew through center of large ball, all 5 small ones, 4 for paws and one for tail.

           (4) Sew tongue, ears and button eyes in place.

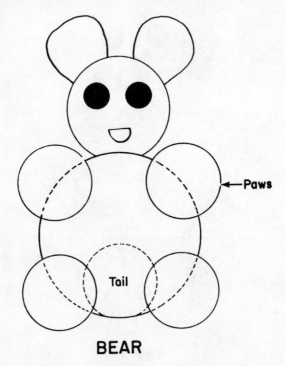

BEAR

Figure 13-9

BEAR

Tongue   Ear

Figure 13-10

Bunny: (1) Make 3 pom-poms, one large (body), one medium (head),
                  and one small (tail).
             (2) Tie large ones together.
             (3) Sew small one through center of large ball for tail.
             (4) Sew on eyes, felt, nose and ears.

Figure 13-11

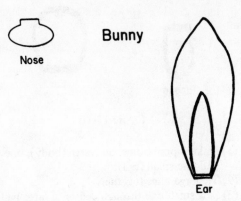

Bunny

Nose

Ear

Figure 13-12

Dog and Cat: These animals can be made in a manner similar to the bear, except for posture and tail. They would stand on all four paws with head and features elevated. Body could be clipped longer in shape. Shape of ears would be according to breed.

Figure 13-13

This project can be adapted for the use of the one-hander by the construction of a jig to hold the cardboard circle while being wound.

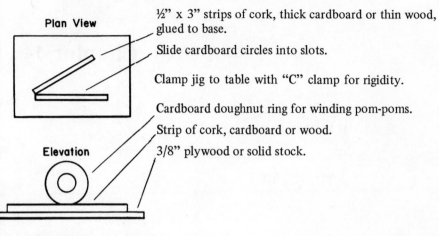

Plan View

½" x 3" strips of cork, thick cardboard or thin wood, glued to base.

Slide cardboard circles into slots.

Clamp jig to table with "C" clamp for rigidity.

Cardboard doughnut ring for winding pom-poms.

Strip of cork, cardboard or wood.

3/8" plywood or solid stock.

Elevation

Figure 13-14

Chapter 14

HAVING FUN
WITH CERAMICS
AND MOSAICS

Ceramic materials, techniques and equipment can be simple or complex. It's wonderful to have your own kiln, glazes, clays and even a wheel on which to "throw" your projects, but none of it is necessary. It takes up room and is expensive. In the average senior citizen center, residence or nursing home there is very little call for such investment in equipment. You may, however, find a volunteer who has it all at home and will supplement your needs as required. What you must know is when it is required for the type of persons you serve.

This is an area where some men show considerable interest, so we try to keep this activity for them. This does not mean women are not welcome to take part. They are, if it is within their interest and ability or needed for specific results. Their projects differ in size and character from those of the men. We locate all mosaic and ceramic supplies in the men's area to encourage them. Most clays and grouts produce soil and discoloration on the skin and clothing, so these materials are worked in the activity room where any messiness can be controlled.

Start with the easiest and simplest forms of modeling materials and equipment. Gradually add skills and techniques.

TYPES OF CLAYS

A. Modeling clay such as the oil base Plasticine does not harden. It is good for hand exercising and manipulation. Three dimensional objects

148

can be shaped for practive and introduction. The results are not permanent.

Figure 14-1

B. Commercial hardening clays come in either powder or wet form. They will harden at room temperature, are usually not waterproof and will look like Mexican pottery in color and texture.

C. Home made clays have been developed from common household ingredients and are very useful. The following are three different recipes and directions.

(1) 1 part cornstarch
2 parts salt
Water to form a paste

(2) Mix 4 Cups flour
1 Cup salt
1½ Cups cold water

Boil ingredients until transparent. To color, use vegetable coloring. Roll out, shape or model into desired form. Will dry hard and strong.

This can be divided into several lots and colored with vegetable coloring. Let it marinate for 1 hour. Model, mould or shape.

These two clays are good for flat Christmas tree ornaments, beads, wall plaques, and decorative items. They are durable.

(3) This clay takes a long time to dry and will be almost as hard as wood. It makes good marionettes and puppet heads.

Mix 1 part dry wall paper paste
8 parts sawdust
2 parts dry ceramic clay
5 parts water

Shape by push and pull method. Allow to dry thoroughly. Paint after dry with tempera paints.

D. Natural pottery clays. These are economical when purchased from a commercial pottery in ten pound lots, ready to use. There are several colors available. A good way to store this clay is in glass jars or covered earthenware crocks. If kept moist, it will last a long time. After shaping and exposing to the air, the clay will become chalk hard and brittle. Firing in a kiln will define the colors, shrink the object slightly and make it more durable. A second firing after glazing will complete the process. If you are interested in preparing your own clay from a ground source, good directions from this process can be found in Reed & Orze, *Art From Scrap,* p. 85. (See bibliography)

TECHNIQUES WITH CLAY

A. *Push and Pull Method*

This is the most basic method for modeling. It can be used with groups or individuals of any age, and clays of any type.

(1) Decide what to make. Here are some general shape suggestions.

        Circle for a chicken, apple or duck

        Square for an elephant or house

        Rectangle for giraffe or person

        Oval for pig or human head

(2) Form general shape first.

(3) Features and details are made by pushing and pulling the general shape into the desired form. Pull arms and legs from the large mass. They must be thick and firm rather than thin and weak. The piece will last longer and be less easily damaged if it is chunky and the parts close together.

Duck: Form ball.

            Elongate by pulling.

            Pull out tail at one end and push upward.

            Pull out head at other end and shape bill with fingers.

            Pull out feet at bottom center. Shape flat and close to body.

            Wings can be pinched and pulled from each side.

            Character of duck is varied by direction of head and position of feet and wings.

Figure 14-2

Beads: Roll clay into balls, round, long, square about 3/4"-1½" in size.

Poke hole through center of bead with nail or knitting needle. Smooth roughness at the hole openings.

Make designs on outside with modeling tools, nails, toothpicks or leather tools.

String on thonging, gimp or fish line with spacers of knots or small beads between.

Poke hole etc.

Make designs etc.   **Figure 14-3**

Figure 14-4

B. *Pinch Pot Method*

1. Make a ball of clay.
2. Push thumb into center.
3. Turn ball of clay around in hand while pressing thumb on inside and fingers on outside, thus thinning the walls. Walls should be uniform thickness.
4. Flatten the bottom by pressing against flat surface.
5. Shape may be round, oblong, tall, squatty, square.

C. *Slab Method*

1. Decide item to be made, such as, tea tile, tray, box, dish.
2. Place lump of clay on hard non-absorbent surface. Have a damp cloth to put over it to keep it moist.
3. Roll out with a rolling pin, piece of dowel or broom handle, to an even thickness. About ½" is good.
4. With knife and ruler, cut bottom piece to shape.
5. Use excess for feet or gallery edges.
6. To fasten two pieces of clay together, a process called "welding" is used. Dip the fingers in water and moisten both pieces of clay where the addition is to fit. Place the addition on the moistened area and smooth the base and addition together inside and outside until it looks as if it were one piece. Handling clay takes the moisture out of it, so hands must be kept moist while welding. If this process is not done well, the item may separate while drying or firing.

Figure 14-5

Box: Make five slabs. Weld together at all corners and edges. A lid may be made from a sixth piece.

Christmas tree ornaments: Roll out and cut with cookie cutter. Paint with food coloring for details and features. Insert a loop of wire at top before allowing to harden.

D. *Coil Method*

1. Decide item to be made: bowl, box, vase.
2. Make base from ½" thick slab of clay, cut to proper shape. Or base may be made formed of continuous coil welded together into desired shape.

Figure 14-6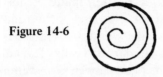

3. To make coil, place lump of clay on non-absorbent surface. Holding hands flat and fingers rigidly straight, roll clay with a back and forth motion until it forms a long coil about ½" in diameter.
4. Moisten the base on top edge and place coil around it, welding together as explained above.
5. Continue to build up sides by adding coils on top of each other and welding together. Occasionally the work must be allowed to dry a bit to hold its shape. Using this method takes longer because of these drying periods.
6. When finished the item may be smoothed on the outside and inside by using water, scraping and sponging.

E. *Making Figures Which Are not Chunky and Squatty*

1. Construct a wire framework of the general shape of the desired figure from coat hanger wire; tack it to a board for stability while working.
2. Press the modeling material into the framework. Papier maché materials may be used on this same frame.
3. Details are made by cutting away with knife or modeling tools.

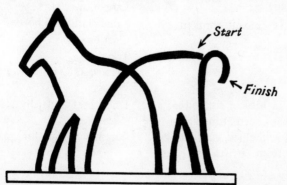

Figure 14-7

For the unusual person, who is experienced in ceramic work, there are bisque figures, already moulded to be painted with glazes and fired in a kiln. Also, there is the potters wheel, either electric or foot operated, upon which larger pieces of pottery are formed. One of these wheels might be borrowed or rented if the need arose.

Good practical information on ceramics is available from local potters and libraries.

MOSAICS

Mosaic is the process of surface decoration made by fastening small pieces of one material to a larger piece of background material. The small pieces can be of paper, glass, tile, wood, plastic, seeds, etc., and the larger backgrounds can be of similar materials. The adhesive can be any glue which is prepared especially for fastening the materials chosen. A final process for making the surface smooth is called grouting and will fill the spaces between the small surface material. This is done with a special grouting powder which forms a paste when mixed with water. It can be colored with tempera paints.

For purposes of use in a senior citizen's center or nursing home, the following ideas we have found practical.

MOSAIC MATERIALS	BACKGROUND MATERIALS
Torn tissue paper, wrapping paper, ornamental paper	Aluminum foil covered boxes
	Cardboard book covers
	Eternal light glass vases
	Plastic containers
Auto windshield glass (rear window) (not sharp when broken—can be dyed with glass dyes)	Pill bottles
	Wooden boxes and forms
	Glass vases
	Plywood (wall collages)
Broken clay pots (can be painted or sprayed with paints—usually not grouted)	Plaques
	Wooden wall plaques
	Large flower pots
Ceramic tiles, mixed, broken or whole)	Large plastic pill bottles
	Cigar boxes
	Trays
	Glass vases
	Bottles
Beach glass or broken colored glass which has been tumbled for smoothing. Stained glass can be secured from artists and glass	Dried beef and jelly glasses (for candles)
	Ceramic forms for plates and bowls

companies
Pebble, smooth from beach or tum-
    bler

Wood—driftwood
Wall plaques
Stepping stones for garden paths

Adhesives: Casein glue for wood paper, tile, glass
Model cement for metal, plastic, glass
Rubber cement for paper
Hardrock water putty for glass stones. From hardware
    stores and lumber yards. Hardens in about 1 hour and
    can be colored with water base paints

Figure 14-8

Chapter 15

PRACTICAL IDEAS IN
NEEDLE AND THREAD

There are very few older women who are not familiar with sewing techniques by the time they have raised a family and become grandmothers. But, not all of them will be able or willing to spend their free time using needle and thread. There will be problems in vision, manual dexterity, mental concentration and interest. So, in most cases, the work you offer in this area will have to have some twist, some unusual appeal, be useful, colorful, and have a definite end direction which they can understand. Above all, it must be within the ability of the senior citizen.

Equipment for practical projects in sewing, embroidery, stitchery and needlework should be acquired slowly as the need arises. One item which is always in use in our workshop is a 1935 treadle sewing machine. The older women feel comfortable with it, since it is "just like one I had at home." The modern zig zag machine is also used, but mostly by staff and volunteers in preparation and completion of projects, construction of therapeutic devices, or tasks of household maintenance. There is an occasional woman who understands the newer electric machine and enjoys using it. We have found the foot control to be the most practical. The knee control is somewhat confusing to older people and stiff hip and knee joints make it difficult to use. Also, if the woman has the need for operating the machine by hand, having no use of her legs, the foot mechanism can be located in an elevated position for elbow control.

When purchasing a sewing machine for use with older people, choose a heavy duty model, with simple features, such as a straight needle and open bobbin winder. Be sure it can be easily oiled, cleaned, and serviced. A sewing machine out of order for any period of time is not worth the room it occupies. Choose carefully when you purchase your mechanical sewing equipment.

Other equipment needed for sewing include the standard items to be found in the sewing basket, chosen for the use of this particular older group. Quality scissors for use with cloth are a must. Buy a good brand, oil them often, and keep them sharp. Stiff hands will find the best of scissors difficult to use. Needles must have long and open eyes to be useful for impaired vision. Often we ask a volunteer to thread a dozen or so needles with white thread and no knots, for ready use by anyone. Pins also can be an aggravation if they are dull,

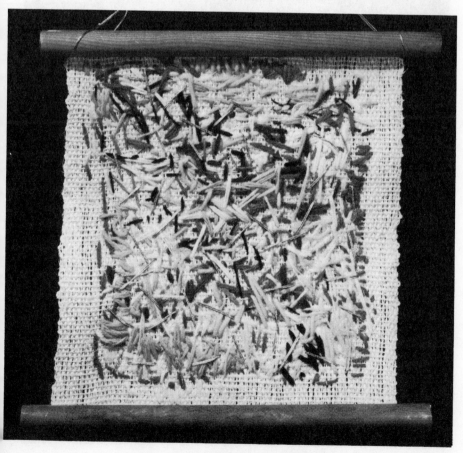

Figure 15-1. Free-Form Crewel Work.

bent, or rusty. Keep supplies of pins in several transparent boxes and also in pincushions, where several may use them at once.

Embroidery, stitchery, and needlework techniques vary widely when applied to the elderly. Background fabrics may be of coarse weave, such as burlap, monk's cloth, or curtain materials. Long, large needles with open eyes of metal or plastic are helpful. Threads can have lots of imagination applied to them; yarns, ribbons, strings, cordings, novelties, seam bindings of any type of fiber make interesting textures in stitchery. Embroidery hoops are useful to keep the material from being drawn up too tightly by lack of coordination in

Figure 15-2. Crewel Embroidery.

pulling the threads. Intricate patterns and lines are hard for the elderly to follow in sewing. Free form crewel work, using color and texture for appeal has been quite successful. A hit or miss method of stitching and novel ways of hanging such work can make very desirable wall decorations and pillow tops. Odds and ends of yarn and small pieces of textured fabrics can be utilized. For one-handers there are embroidery hoops which clamp to the table or chair arm. These are foreign made and available from the Preston Company* and local department stores.

Simple, large-patterned areas of crewel work can be done by some senior citizens. Here again, color contrast helps, and line direction will make an effective and usable piece of work.

Two tricks we have used to make threading yarn needles easier and joining yarns more effective and less obvious are:

- *Threading needles.* Fold the yarn over the needle, hold tightly between the fingers and pull the needle out. Open the fingers gradually and, while still holding the yarn flat, push it through the eye of the needle

- *Joining old and new yarn together.* Place the new yarn on the right and the old yarn, which is attached to the work, on the left. Thread the new yarn onto the needle. Insert the needle 3" in from the end of the old yarn, and weave in and out toward the work for 3". Remove needle and pull yarn back slightly, until end disappears. Thread the 3" end of the old yarn onto needle. At the point where the first thread was woven in, insert the needle and weave in and out in the opposite direction for 3" or the length of the end. Both ends should disappear into the yarn. There will be a slight bulge, but it will not come apart.

Figure 15-3

The following projects have been successful with elderly women and have originated from the use of discarded and donated materals.

APRONS

1. *Basic Five Piece Apron.*
   - Tear pieces for straightness, then iron
   - Measurements allow for ½" seams.
   - Body of apron, 20" x 40"; make 3" hem at bottom.

*See Bibliography.

- Waist band, 15" long and 7" wide.
- 2 ties, 16" x 3", turn hems on 2 long and 1 short side.
- 1 pocket 6" x 6".

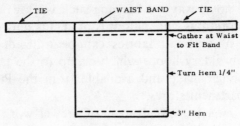

Figure 15-4

2. *Burlap Patio Apron.*

- Salvage potato sacks from the kitchen.
- Open bag by ripping double chain stitch. (To rip chain stitch, hold the single thread side of the bag toward you. Start at the right side, cut 2 stitches.

  Take hold of the front thread in one hand and the rear thread in the other. Pull apart the full length of end and side of the bag.)
- Wash bag to remove stains and even out color.
- Salvage a 20" x 40" piece of material.
- Machine stitch a single row 2" inside all 4 sides of the piece.
- Fringe all 4 sides up to the stitching.
- Having fringe on front side, turn down one long side; make a 2" casing for the tie ribbon at the waist.
- Use bright worsted to fasten casing and for embroidery on the apron.
- Threads may be pulled and replaced with bright yarn.
- Pass a 42" ribbon through the casing.
- Monk's cloth can be used in the same manner.

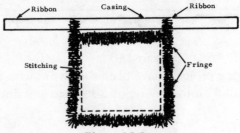

Figure 15-5

3. *Apron of Squares.*

- Cut 4" or 5" squares of washable material.
- Stitch either by hand or machine, into strips.
- Stitch strips together into 20" x 40" oblong.
- Use instructions for basic apron to complete.

4. *Strip Aprons.*

- Cut or tear strips 4" or 5" wide and 20" long.
- Stitch together by hand or machine with strips going up and down.
- Use instructions for basic apron to complete.

Decorative pillows and afghans may be made by these same methods, using small amounts of materials, discards, and donations. Oriental knotting, fringe and ball fringe may be used as decorations and edging on pillows.

DECORATIONS MADE OF CLOTH AND YARN

Wool Flowers.

These provide decorations for burlap aprons or pillows, or similar pieces. You will need a pencil, green yarn for the stem, and colored yarn for the flower. Cut the green yarn 12" long and the colored yarn into 24" lengths. Lay the green yarn along the length of the pencil and secure ends with tape. Wrap the colored yarn around the diameter of the pencil from left to right, keeping the loops close together. When the colored yarn is used up, draw the green yarn up from either side, holding the colored yarn tightly to prevent unwrapping. Slide the pencil away and tie the green yarn in a square knot. This will form a ring of colored yarn loops. You may add a center with a large yellow knot. Wire may be used in place of the green yarn, but it is harder to handle. Larger flowers may be made on larger diameter doweling.

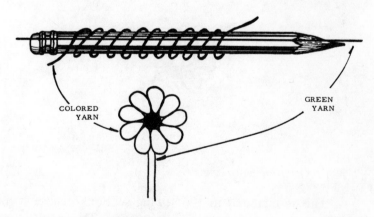

COLORED YARN

GREEN YARN

Figure 15-6

Flowers from fringed cloth squares. Cut several 3" squares of brightly colored cloth. Fringe all four sides. Make a small hole through the center of each. Using flexible wire wind it around a small artificial flower or stamen and insert this through the hole to make center for the flower. Use several different colors of squares rotated to make a circle. Wrap the stem with floral tape.

Flowers from Bright Burlap.

Cut burlap in pieces 8" x 4". Pull all of the long threads out of the center, leaving a 1" border of material on each long edge. Use the pulled out threads for the flower centers by gluing one end of the bunch together with casein glue. Fold the unravelled edges of the burlap together, thus making the ravelled portion into loops for petals. Using a #20 florists' wire, fold over the top 6" of the wire and lay the loop end in next to the center on the burlap. Glue the center wire on one end of the unravelled burlap edge and roll it toward the other end, using glue as you roll. The tighter you roll, the tighter the flower. Wind the base of the flower with florists' tape, continuing down the wire stem.

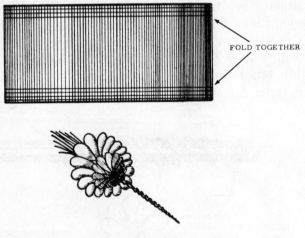

FOLD TOGETHER

Figure 15-7

Oriental Knotting.

This is included in the sewing section because it most always involves some sewing to put it to use. The resulting fringe type material can be used as stuffed animal manes, edging on pillows, aprons, and can be made into mats and rugs. There are many ways to accomplish this process, and a description of it is included in Jean Wilson's *Weaving Is For Everyone,* on pp. 131-134. However, we have made some adaptations for our special needs, and observations from the senior citizens' point of view.

We tie single oriental knots on an upright frame, which holds two vertical threads. This frame can be clamped to a table or chair arm for stability in operation. The length of the fringe can be short or long, according to need.

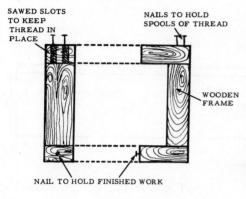

SAWED SLOTS TO KEEP THREAD IN PLACE

NAILS TO HOLD SPOOLS OF THREAD

WOODEN FRAME

NAIL TO HOLD FINISHED WORK

To form the knot, hold the center of the 3" yarn across the front of the two vertical threads. Pass the two ends to the back, behind the threads and pull through to the front between the threads, below the loop. Push down toward the nail. Successive knots formed this way will make the fringe.

When starting, tie the two threads together under the nail, and leave 3"-4" end for later use.

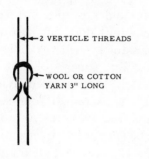

2 VERTICLE THREADS

WOOL OR COTTON YARN 3" LONG

Figure 15-8

This fringe may be sewed together in strips, or back and forth to make a rug. We have found that it does not work well if sewed together in a circle or oval. It is very difficult to ease enough on the ends to have the rug lie flat.

For cutting the short pieces of material for the knots, there is a cardboard jig. A double-folded piece of cardboard, 8" x 3" before folding, is used. Wind the material around the cardboard the short way and cut at the open edge.

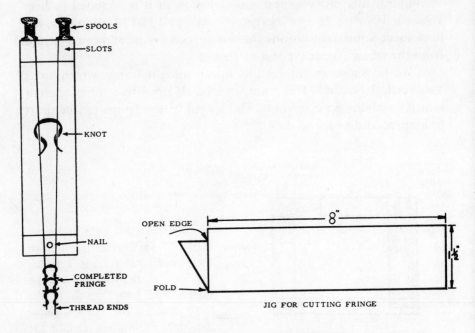

Figure 15-9   **Figure 15-10**

Quilts, if not too large, are a good group project. Fancy patterns are, as a rule, too complicated for older people, but a simple square or triangle pattern is useful. Be sure it does not become tedious. A baby quilt we have found successful is made as follows: For each square of the quilt you will need 2-6" squares of patterned or plain cotton, or cotton flannel material, 1 clean used nylon hose, and embroidery thread. Turn in ¼" hems on all four sides of the 2 squares of cloth. Blanket stitch the two squares together, hems inside, right sides out, leaving one side open. Arrange the nylon hose as if to put it on. Starting at the top, catch it all the way up to the toe. It will have a circular shape, with the toe in the middle, and the top around the outside. Slide the hose in this position into the open pocket formed by the two squares of cloth. Tack these together through the center, fastening the nylon. Blanket stitch the open side. Thirty or thirty-five squares will make a good sized crib blanket, when whipped together into strips and the strips put together. An edging is not necessary, but a crocheted border finishes it nicely. Sometimes we sew balls from ball fringe at the intersections of the squares. This gives it a finished look.

The felt clip-on mouse, used as a "cheerer-upper" will bring happiness to many senior citizens. It takes very little material and effort, but will have to be the project of an unusually capable person who can handle five small pieces of felt, one hair clip, and three beads, (2 for eyes and 1 for nose.)

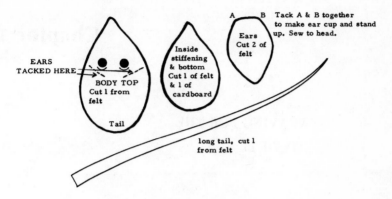

A   B   Tack A & B together
          to make ear cup and stand
Ears   up. Sew to head.
Cut 2 of
felt

Inside
stiffening
& bottom
Cut 1 of felt
& 1 of
cardboard

EARS
TACKED HERE

BODY TOP
Cut 1 from
felt

Tail

long tail, cut 1
from felt

Figure 15-11

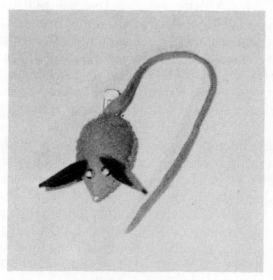

Figure 15-12

Sew body top and bottom together by hand with the cardboard bottom inserted. Leave small opening at tail to stuff with small amount of cotton. (Save cotton from pharmacy bottles.) Insert one side of hair clip on bottom outside of the mouse. Tack tail in same area and close opening with thread and needle. Sew on ears and eyes. Contrasting bright colors of felt scraps are used in this project.

Chapter 16

WEAVING FOR THE
JOY OF IT

An Activity Program Director will usually have to work hard to convince an elderly person that there is a type of weaving which is within his ability and interest. The senior citizen will remember the complicated, fancy, and time-consuming looms which he, as a child, saw operated by his aunt or grandmother. This chapter will deal with the simple looms, weaving techniques, materials, ideas and adaptations necessary for the use of the majority of our senior citizens.

Curiosity, interest, and devotion will have to be in the mind of an older person who wants to learn to weave from scratch. However, if that person is ill, or has a physical disability, certain adjustments in the operation of the loom will be needed. Some of the aged can make these changes themselves; mainly the Activity Program Director will have to be aware of these needs in order to help as they arise.

For example, the grandmother recovering from a stroke which has paralyzed her dominant hand, can be taught to do simple weaving. Her good hand helps her paralyzed one with the passing of the shuttle through the shed and the operation of the beater to set the firmness of the completed fabric. Actually she does only the weaving, none of the preparation of the loom which must precede this operation. Many residents will never be able to master the complicated winding of a warp and putting it onto the loom. Likewise, they may never be able to learn the steps necessary for the removal of the completed fabric from the loom. Curiosity, interest, and devotion here are coupled with the desire to return the dominant hand to as near normal use as possible.

At other times, the desire to make some attractive and useful piece to be given as a gift motivates an elderly person to learn the process of weaving. Be sure the outcome is attractive, bright and gay in color, and big and bold in the design. The simpler the equipment and directions are, the better for all concerned.

TABLE LOOMS

There are many kinds, sizes, and types of table looms. The simplest one which is still practical has a 12" weaving area, two harnesses, one change of shed, and is operated manually. A sturdy, well-built loom of this type can be secured for about $20.00 from Handicrafters, Waupun, Wisconsin, 53963. It is light in weight and will have to be fastened with either "C" clamps, spring type clamps, or sand bag weights to a table surface or lap board, especially if the operator has any kind of physical or personality stress which can easily produce irritation.

For this loom, a straight, flat shuttle is best. Be sure that it is at least as wide as the weaving, with deeply grooved ends. When winding the material onto it, fasten the beginning of the thread at one end with tape to hold it firmly while the weaver winds it.

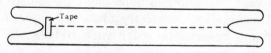

Figure 16-1

Clamp this small loom to a portable type T.V. tray, or table with legs to be easily moved about where the weaver wishes to work.

WARP:

This loom will hold at least five yards of warp, usually 100 to 110 threads wide. When winding any warp for beginning weavers, place a linen thread or two on both outside borders to form a firm selvaged edge, which will not break if pulled in too tightly.

The best materials to use in a warp for a beginner are: carpet warp, heavy crochet thread, cotton, or linen warping materials. Refrain from using wool warps. Several colors which are compatable can be wound alternately in stripes, with a formal balanced pattern or repetitive colors in sequence. Warp materials and textures may vary, and will be attractive in the end result. Methods of winding warps are given in detail in many weaving books, some of which are listed in the last chapter. We shall not give formal directions, just suggestions for making the warp successful for new weavers. Do not try to put on a warp alone. The best even tension can be achieved with two people working. Try to convin ce the interested resident to be the second person. The experienced person should work at the warp beam end, where lengths of the warp threads can be affected markedly and easily if the tension and flat winding is not maintained.

WEFT OR WOOF

Weft or woof materials can truly show imagination. They can be fine or coarse, of natural or artificial fibers—ribbons (plain and also the corrugated Christmas type), strings, cotton, wool, linen, sticks, grasses, and pipe cleaners. We have used as accents tongue blades, raffia, cat tail leaves, reeds, lolly-pop sticks, swamp and beach grasses, cedar bark, reclaimed yarn, novelty and homespun knitting wools. The choice of the right and proper material for the individual is the trick. A person with adventure in his soul will love to experiment with some of the unusual materials listed, but the more conventional person will want to keep with the old and well-known favorites.

One 93 year old, who had done many place mats of washable, conventional materials wished to try a new technique. We started her on a ribbon wall hanging, in which wide ribbons were to be split down the middle before weaving. This went fine until it came to actually weaving them into the warp. Part of the charm of this texture is the fuzzy thread look after it is woven, and the edge fringe formed by the short pieces of ribbon. But, her prim nature and desire for the conventional look she was used to, made her upset and so nervous that she became temporarily disenchanted with weaving in general.

Be careful with your choice of weft materials. Continuously wound shuttles make the best weft for learning. Start with a single color until the process is familiar, and then introduce two and three colors or textures, each wound on a separate shuttle. Be sure to watch your edges. Each color should be passed through the shed at least two times to keep the edge threads firmly woven.

Materials made on this narrow a loom have many uses when completed. A partial list would include travel kits to hold hosiery and jewelry, wall hangings, place mats, tea towels, clutch bags, work bags, eye glass cases, book covers, or pillow tops. Patterns for travel kit and eye glass case will be found later in this chapter.

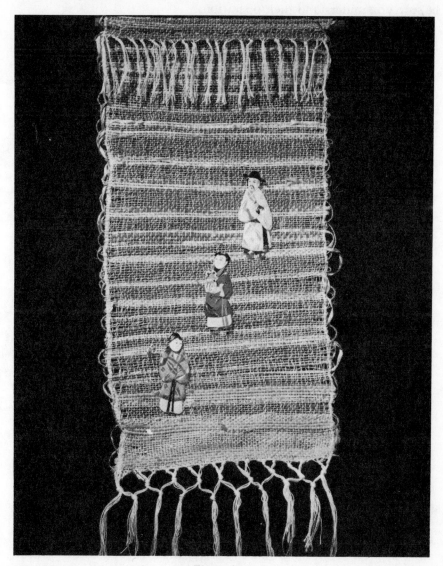

Figure 16-2

Wider table looms of two and four harnesses are practical for
rograms for senior citizens. But, we
two since they take up room and lots
)nly the very well resident will be able

to master the technicalities of pattern weaving which is the virtue of a four harness loom. The wider floor looms also are a space problem. So, think twice before you invest in these larger types of looms, and be sure you understand their operation.

BICYCLE WHEEL OR HOOP LOOM

This type of loom, in several sizes and designs, is pictured and described in *Weaving Is For Everyone,* by Jean Wilson. We would suggest that warping materials other than cloth be used on this loom, with a variety of end results in mind. Any warp should be very strong and firm; Belfast cord is excellent. You will thread the warp through the empty spoke holes on the rim, and cross in the center of the wheel to the opposite side. Be sure that there is an uneven number of warp threads when finished. To do this the weaver may have to draw two warp threads together as one. In the finished work this will not show.

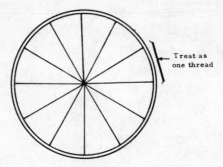

Figure 16-3

Use strips of cloth, rug yarn, raffia, or any good sized material for weaving. For the first inner one inch you may want to use a fine weft to make a firm start. Starting in the center, weave over one and under one alternately, overlapping or tying in a square knot when starting a new piece of weft. Other texture weaves may be used, such as over one and under two warp threads. Weave to within 2" of the metal rim, using the remainder of the warp thread to tie together in pairs to prevent raveling. Cut two warp threads apart, on the outside of the rim, remove them from the hole and tie in a square knot tightly against the weft inside the rim. Continue this around the outside of the edge of the work, which may be finished with fringe or binding. If a wool weft is used, do not pull too tightly when weaving or the finished product will "dish" and not lie flat. If this happens, make it into a stuffed pillow.

Products from this type of loom may be used in many ways. It is wise to have in mind what your end result will be while you are weaving. Results can be chair seats, mats, round table covers, place mats, hot dish mats, drawstring bags, and many other round usable items.

An adventurous, curious spirit will enjoy weaving on a round loom. It takes nimble fingers and pretty good eyesight, but it is unusual and worth trying.

Figure 16-4

The loom is made from an empty wooden wire reel. Metal reels are not as adaptable, because slots must be sawn in the top and bottom discs, opposite each other for holding the warp threads in place. There must be an odd number of warp threads, thus an odd number of slots. Here, as previously, the warp material must be firm and not easily frayed, since it gets much handling as the weaving takes place. Four ply knitting worsteds, rug yarns, or Belfast cord would make good warp materials. The weft materials must be compatable to the warp—fine for fine, coarse for coarse—and a heading of some fine, firm, and durable material should first be woven, about 1" wide. With this loom, as with the wheel loom and other finger weaving looms, different patterns of over and under warp thread can be used. Some of the basketry patterns are very adaptable here and very effective. Reels of any size can be used for this loom. The one pictured here is 14" high and 10" in diameter. However, smaller ones such as lampshades, make interesting projects. Use a springy type warp which does not slip, since there are no sawed slots to hold it in place.

A very small scale round loom can be made on a disposable cardboard ribbon spool, but I would not recommend it for the average weaver. It would be too fine and nerve-racking. Keep it in mind for the unusually curious and able person.

To remove the material from the loom, simply slip the loops of the warp off the edges of the slots on both ends. They are all continuous and it will not fray out. If you have pushed it down very tightly as it was woven, the slight looseness at the top will not be noticeable. It will be taken up by the tension as the material is worked into a useful item. Work material off the round flat top by easing from side to side and sliding it up and off. Items made from this tube-like piece of cloth can be pillows, balls, work bags, drawstring bags, and ski caps.

FOUR, SIX, AND EIGHT-SIDED HAND LOOMS

This is a reference to the Flat Looper and Weavit frames. Picture frames and cardboard weaving devices can be used to obtain the same results—individually woven small pieces which are in turn sewn together to make useful projects. The small, fine work involved is for the very dexterous and capable person. Each gathering place where residents work should have one or two of these looms on hand.

The products can be made into pot holders or they can be assembled into baby pillows, bibs, or blankets.

Other finger, needle and hook weaving has been effectively done on many materials. One is "Punchinello" ribbon; the product resulting from the punching out of sequins. It is a long metallic roll of ventilated ribbon, which is easily cut into sizes and shapes. We have woven threads, yarn, and other ribbons through the holes in patterns, some hit or miss, others planned. These result in book marks, place mats, and bell cords.

Mesh cloth weaving can be done on lacy drapery fabrics, burlap with pulled threads, dish cloths, squared canvas materials, and red onion bags. Weaving of this type takes fairly good eyesight, and ability to follow a line of holes created by the drawing out of threads in an order or pattern. Some of the drapery fabrics come as discontinued samples from upholstery firms, and are large enough to make sets of place mats and small table covers. If the openwork pattern is large enough, try running bias tape, or seam binding in bright colors through it for an unusual result. The red onion bags, from the institution's kitchen, usually need some preparation before they are ready to use. The paper label will need to be soaked off, the bag stitching ripped open on two sides, and some ironing and straightening of the fibers. If you prepare this material for place mats, the use of masking tape on the edges before the binding is stitched on will hold the fibers from fraying. With the red background and bright primary colors of cotton yarn run through in a border pattern, these have a gay, Mexican look.

In planning weaving projects for the elderly, be constantly alert to new materials, techniques, and ideas.

DIRECTIONS FOR MAKING A TRAVEL KIT

(a) 1-8½" x 11" piece of handweaving or upholstery fabric for outside.

(b) 1-8½" x 11" piece of felt in compatable color for lining.

(c) 2-6" Zippers.

(d) 2-8½" x 1" felt strips to match lining.

- Fold both items (d) in half lengthwise and zig zag two times lengthwise for strength. When sewn in place these will hold earrings and pins.
- Following layout pattern, open felt lining for the two zippers 1¼" down from the top and 6" down from the top. Stitch zippers in slits.
- Stitch the two felt strips at 7" and 9" down from the top, three times, once in center and once at each end.

- Place lining and outside right sides together and stitch three edges together using 3/8" seams. Leave bottom short edge open for turning.
- Turn right side out. Press well, hand stitch bottom edge and machine stitch center, just above lower zipper.
- Sew three snaps in place.

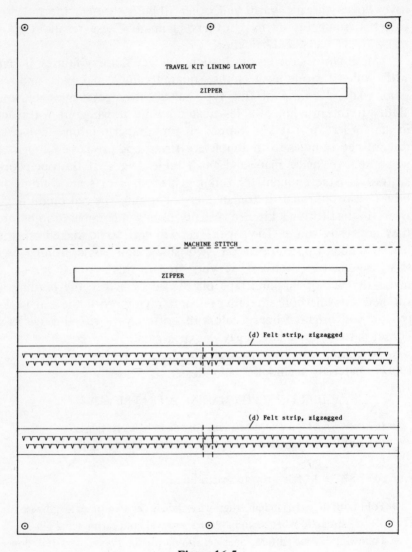

Figure 16-5

GLASSES CASE

(a) Cut two pieces of material 7¼" x 8". One is for lining and one for outside.

(b) Stitch together (right sides together). Leave corner open for turning.

(c) Turn, press. Fold in center as marked.

(d) Turn in area left open for turning, and sew closed.

(e) Sew together portion marked "sew." Leave open portion marked "open."

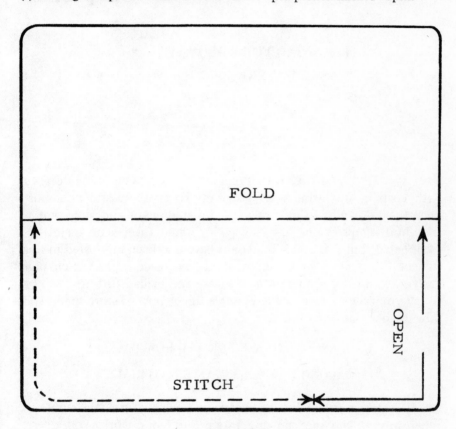

FOLD

OPEN

STITCH

Figure 16-6

Chapter 17

PLANNING FOR ADEQUATE

WASTE MATERIALS

   As an Activity Program Director, you are concerned with costs of operating your program. To be successful you must keep them down by using discarded, donated, waste and scrap materials. Activity programs have always operated from large quantities of donated items. Individual artisans have also been interested in this subject. There are good books which I have listed in the last chapter for you to use for stimulation of ideas. The main effort here will be to tell you how to acquire these usable items, how to store them, and how to go about using them.

WHAT TO ASK FOR AND HOW TO

ACQUIRE USEABLE WASTE MATERIALS

   Develop a guide list of materials you can use. Distribute it generously to anyone showing interest in your work: volunteers, residents' families, employees, and friends. The following is the list we use:

OLD NYLON HOSE	NAILS, SCREWS
CLOTH-12" SQUARE OR LARGER	YARN, WOOL OR COTTON
RIBBON, RICKRACK, TAPE, LACE	SCRAPS OF WOOD, DOWEL-
FELT	ING
ELASTIC	GOOD BOOKS AND PAPER-
SPOOLS	BACKS
PINS AND NEEDLES	OLD DOLLS TO RENEW AND
BUTTONS, BEADS, TRIMS	REDRESS

THREAD: SEWING AND EM- BROIDERY PAPER, COLORED CARDBOARD, LARGE PIECES	BINGO PRIZES, NOVELTIES, & WHITE ELEPHANTS SIMPLE PATTERNS FOR APRONS AND STUFFED TOYS

As you develop contacts in this area, you will be deluged with materials, some of which you never considered usable. The strange thing is that you *will* use them. We use old movie film and cellophane tape reels for toy wheels. Short sections of discarded telephone cable are taken apart and used for lacing and decorations in place of gimp. Rear windshield glass, when broken, does not cut older, tender skin. We use it in mosaics.

There are numerous sources of materials which you may solicit. This is in addition to the interested persons' voluntary contributions.

- *Local printer or newspaper*—paper trimmings, offset metal sheets, newsprint rolls, cardboard.
- *Upholstery shops*——wallpaper and drapery samples, upholstery fabrics, webbing, foam rubber.
- *Lumber yards, cabinet shops*—wood scraps of all sizes.
- *Construction projects*—all manner of materials.
- *Clothing manufacturers*—cloth and fabric pieces, Dacron stuffing and trimmings.
- *Ceramic tile dealers*—broken tiles for ceramic work.
- *Retail stores*—discarded and discontinued items, shopworn goods.
- *Insurance companies*—song books and record service books.
- *Newspapers and magazines*—designs, pictures and ideas, coupons for premiums.
- *Vacations*—beach, meadow, and woods combings.

ACKNOWLEDGING RECEIPT OF MATERIALS

The "thank you's" for donations are the job of the Activity Program Director, and are classed as No. 1 public relations. Personal notes or a telephone call will pay off in future interests. Keep a record of who donates what, if for no other reason than the sending of a Christmas card. Another method of acknowledgement is to be sure the donor knows what happens to his contributions. This may encourage more interest in your activity program.

SORTING AND STORING.

The sorting, storing, and in some cases, preparing for use, of the donated goods takes up a considerable amount of the Activity Director's time, or perhaps that of a volunteer, if this is feasible. However, it is difficult to know what materials are on hand if you have not looked them over yourself. As you investigate, be thinking of applications for use, in which project, and by whom. Show something unusual to the residents. They will have ideas—and good ones, too. Also, as you sort, organize the preparation of projects for the residents to do. Such jobs as the ironing of cloth, ribbons, papers, and the rejuvenating of yarns, soaking off of labels, sorting of buttons, snaps, hooks, beads, tape, rickrack, lace, etc., are all part of the department operation and contribute to a first-class, end result.

If storage space is adequate, many items which may be used in the future can be kept, but a good rule of thumb is to discard anything which is not used after six months.

Egg cartons and molded candy box liners make good sorting trays for small items such as buttons, beads, snaps, and the like.

In reclaiming used yarn a yarn swift or niddy-noddy will be a useful piece of equipment. On them you can wind skeins to prepare yarn for washing and then re-using.

Store like items together. As a suggestion, all materials used for mending and repairing clothing, all knitting and crocheting and weaving materials and equipment should be in one area, close together. Follow this system throughout.

Mark and label boxes plainly with black on white. A felt tipped pen is good for this. When you have time, go over the supplies, review what is on hand, continually sort and question use for each item. Don't get buried under useless materials.

HOW TO USE WASTE MATERIALS

One hundred percent absorption of donated waste materials into the activity program depends upon a creative, ingenious, and sharing nature of the person in charge. Give other people a chance to be exposed to the materials with which you need help.

Some suggestions are:

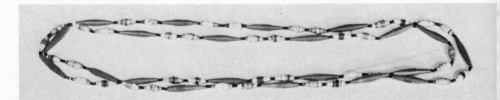

Figure 17-1

Felt or paper rolled beads (see photograph).

Rolled colored paper tubes to decorate wastebaskets, crayon boxes.

Spools for stringing, dolls, build up into toys, trees, for use as feet on boxes and tiles.

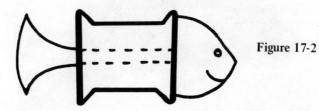

Figure 17-2

Metal pull tabs, from pop cans, picture hangers, long strings, hooked together for Christmas tree ornaments, use in place of bone rings.

Stone and *pebble* people and animals.

Beads and *broken jewelry*—decorations on animals and toys.

Cone trees and animals (see photographs).

Figure 17-3A

Figure 17-3B

Figure 17-4

Shell aninals, plaques and collages (Figure 17-4).
Driftwood—wind chimes, wall plaques (see photograph).

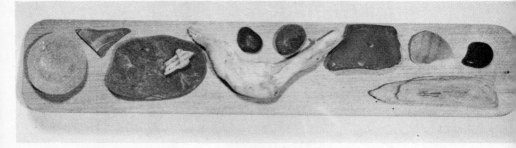

Figure 17-5

Pomander Balls: Materials: Oranges or apples.
                                        Cloves.
                                        Cinnamon.
                                        Orris root powder.
                                        Ribbon, 36" long, one for each fruit.

Directions: Wipe fruit with disinfectant.

Stick it solidly with cloves.

Let dry over night.

Shake in a paper bag containing equal parts orris root and cinnamon.

Tie ribbon around body of fruit 2 times and hang to season.

These are old-fashioned and have a luscious aroma.

Birthday Medallion: Save ribbons from discarded plants or gift wrappings. Iron smooth. Cut ribbons into 5" lengths and choose colors which blend. Cut a 3" circle from cardboard. Fold the ribbons in half and staple the cut ends to the cardboard circle so that the loops extend beyond the perimeter. The edge of the cardboard should not show. The number of loops of ribbon needed will vary according to the ribbon width. If the rosette is to be pinned on, make one loop longer and use a safety pin. To cover the ends of the ribbon in the center use circles of colored or metallic paper or lace doilies.

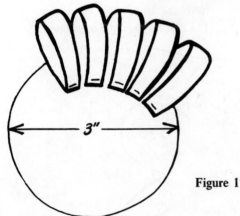

Figure 17-6

Pill Bottle Plant Tags: Save pill bottles which have straight sides and moisture proof snap-on tops. Remove the labels. Place a strip of heavy paper inside for recording plant name. Replace the cap. Cut an 8" strip of plastic coated wire from discarded telephone cable. Twist the wire around the neck of the bottle in the groove just below the cap. Leave ends long enough for tying to plant or shrub. This is a good project for men.

Cloth Flowers: Materials: White iron-on cloth.
                                Gingham cotton fabric.
                                Beads or buttons.
                                8" pieces of #20 florist's wire.
                                Green florist's tape.

                     Directions: Make a cardboard pattern for the petals
                                Following directions for the iron-on
                                cloth, put the two fabrics together. Cut
                                out the flowers, using the pattern. Cut
                                a "Y" in the center. Wire the bead or
                                button by passing the wire through the
                                holes and doubling it the full 4" length.
                                This is the flower center. Put the wired
                                center through the "Y" and use floral
                                tape to cover the wire, winding it diag-
                                onally from the top down. If you wish
                                more shape to the flower, use a stapler
                                where the dotted lines appear on the
                                pattern. Fold petal upward along dotted
                                line, right sides together, and staple
                                from the back along the dotted line.
                                The staples should not show in front.

Figure 17-7

Powder Box: Materials: 1 round plastic liquid soap container.
                                Beads, buttons, rick-rack for trim.
                                Plastic glue.
                                Sharp knife and scissors.

Directions: Cut off top of container at widest point above center. Discard center portion. Cut off bottom at narrow part. The top will fit over the bottom to complete the box. The cap may make an attractive knob, or cut off threading at top and cover with button or bead to make a knob. Decorate the box with rick-rack.

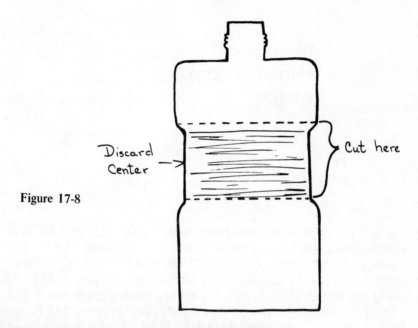

Figure 17-8

Figure 17-9

Chapter 18

PROJECTS OF
PARTICULAR INTEREST
TO MEN

FOR MEN ONLY

It's the exception rather than the rule to find an elderly man who wants to be busy with projects. Mostly he just wants to sit and rest. "I've worked all my life," he'll say, "Now I'm going to watch." Let him! Give him the opportunity to see things going on, things other people do, things other people make. Kidnap him! Take him on a tour of the facility, and be sure that he knows the schedule of activities. Have him know what is available, where the books are, where and when refreshments are served, where the cards and puzzles are kept and when games are played. It may take several weeks, but if he calls you "slave driver" you've won him over to the program. He's paying attention.

A very fine line exists between reviving old skills and renewing a patient's interest in former activities. To try to revive old skills can be defeating because of lost abilities. A family will say, "Dad used to do anything and everything with wood. He could make anything he wanted to." That's fine, but he "used to." His hands, eyes, energy and drive have changed. To try to do the same type of projects could discourage and depress him. But, if you kindle his interest in wood and woodworking by suggesting that he sand children's building blocks of different sizes and shapes, which have been pre-cut, then you are renewing his interest in his former hobby without expecting the perfect end result to which he was accustomed when he was younger.

Figure 18-1

When we were constructing the addition to Issaquah Villa, we went out daily to the site of the construction, picking up small blocks of lumber and oddly shaped pieces of cedar and birch. These have been used to construct small wooden pull toys—trolley cars, train engines, autos and wagons. A volunteer cut wheels on his band saw. We also have used empty magnetic tape and movie film spools, scotch tape containers or thread spools. Constructing and painting useful and colorful toys such as these can be satisfying for some men.

Figure 18-2

Figure 18-3

Wall Plaques of Wood.

Men can prepare and finish the backing plate for wall plaques of natural materials, beach combings or driftwood. Soft woods of pine and cedar will be easier to work with for those with less than normal energy, than the harder woods of maple, birch or oak.

You may have a whittler whose products can be used. This takes a special talent and materials. Pine, balsa, and freshly cut alder are woods easily shaped with a sharp knife. Be sure your whittler has a steady hand and all his thinking power. Cuts in older people are slow to heal. In assembly, contrast of materials and tones adds to the attractiveness.

Figure 18-4

Wall Plaques of Mosaic

Designs of seahorses, starfish, and other fish can be cut from masonite or ¼" plywood on a jig saw or by hand saw. These are covered with broken clay pots, ceramic tiles or windshield glass by gluing the pieces close together and letting them overlap the edges a bit. When the surface is completely covered with the irregular material, and dried, it can be painted with lamp black, dry tempera, or sprayed with black enamel. Other colors may be used but they should be dark to cover thē irregularity. A highlighting of gold or silver from a spray can gives some life to the end result. Use a button or commercial eye, properly glued in place, and tack a hanger on the back. Barnyard animals are also interesting done in this same fashion. Suggestions will develop. Grab them up quickly and put them into operation. This is how to keep a man's interest.

Figure 18-5

Wall Plaques With Tacks

The same designs can be decorated with ornamental upholstery tacks to emphasize fins, scales, wings and facial features. This is a noisy operation, but for the men it is fun!

Refinishing Relics

For the men who like to reminisce, bring in some old hames, singletrees, or wagon wheels to be refinished. They have lots of fun remembering their contacts of years gone by while sanding, filling and finishing these relics. You might even contact an antique shop to do some of this work for them.

Encourage the men to organize and keep the woodworking portion of the workroom in good order. They will enjoy putting up a peg board for hanging tools in full view and within reach. Contact paper, cut to the shape of the tools, and mounted on the peg board will tell you at a glance which one is in use or missing.

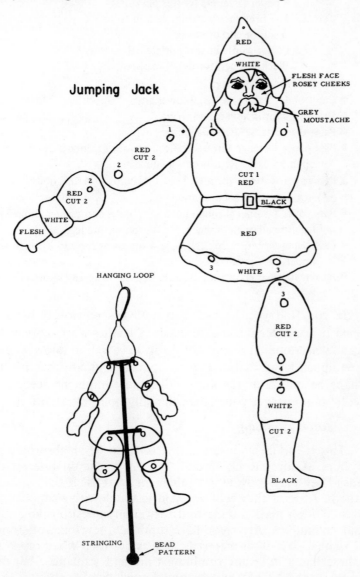

Figure 18-6

JUMPING JACKS OF WOOD OR CARDBOARD

These can be made for decorations or useful toys. The designs can be for girls or boys—ballerinas, soldiers, clowns, Humpty Dumpty, teddy bear, etc. The general directions for cutting, assembling and stringing the Santa Claus Jumping Jack are:

Materials: 1/8" wood of bass or mahogany, or heavy cardboard.
        8 paper fasteners (cotter pin type)
        15" heavy duty string, dark in color
        Bead for end of string
        Poster paints in appropriate colors
        Black felt pen for detail markings

Directions for assembling:
- Cut 1 body, 2 upper arms, 2 lower arms, 2 upper legs, 2 lower legs.
- Drill holes for fasteners and string.
- Paint the parts before assembling.
- Pass paper fastener through hole 2 of lower arm and upper arm. Spread open on back. Repeat on second arm.
- Pass paper fastener through hole 1 of upperarm and body. Spread open on back, repeat on second arm.
- Pass paper fastener through hole 3 on body, and through hole 3 of lower leg. Spread open on back. Repeat on second leg.
- Pass paper fastener through hole 4 on lower leg and through hole 4 of upper leg. Spread open at back.
- Fasten string as shown on diagram with non-slipping knots. (Figures 18-6, 7)

If you find you have a man who has previously been accomplished in some technical skill, such as leather work, copper tooling, origami, macrame, and can still do it, it is well to know where to go for equipment and materials to encourage and continue his interest. Perhaps he has all of the knowledge and equipment needed. In this case, let him instruct you. This will really hold his attention.

Rock Tumbling

This is the men's interest area and can be an absorbing activity for them. A local Rock Hound club may take an interest in your needs. They may provide a tumbler for your use if the request is put to them. At least they will put you in touch with a supplier of grits, hulls and other needed items and answer any questions you may have about techniques. After you have tumbled a few loads of stones, you will want to try other materials such as petrified wood or glass. Each of these has a different tumbling time and sequence. Let the men read up on this process and become knowledgeable about it. You can get some instruction manuals and books from the library.

Find things to do with the resulting products. A nice round

Figure 18-7

smooth stone can be a "pocket piece," once called an "Executive Pacifier," in a pants pocket to be fingered by a nervous hand. The Rock Club may like to have the polished stones to sell at their shows. (They loan the tumbler and you return the product.) This is a good way to make solid community relations and have understanding of your program at the same time. Flower arrangers also use these polished stones in their art. Unusually attractive pieces can be assembled into tie tacks, key rings, and earrings.

In working with older men, we have learned that they need a variety of activities from which they may choose. Sometimes they will work a bit on one and move to another job; keep the paths open to them at all times with friendly encouragement.

Chapter 19

DISPLAYING PRODUCTS
AND MAKING SIGNS

If no one knows what has been accomplished or what is to happen, the fame of the activity department is in jeopardy. Well made signs, posters, newsletters and displays will help start you on this road to fame.

SIGNS AND POSTERS

These are as necessary as word-of-mouth advertising. Three features will make a sign an attention-getter, attractive and pleasing to read: (1) keep it simple; (2) make it easy to read; (3) give it shock value.

(1) Keep It Simple.
- (a) Use few colors, such as black, white and one color.
- (b) State only the necessary facts. Make the message direct.
- (c) Keep the shape conventional, not confusing.
- (d) Consider the area where the sign will be displayed. Make it big enough to attract attention but not so big that it is in the way. Counter top size, 8"-10" wide, 14"-18" high.

(2) Easy to Read.
- (a) Use large, clear and distinct letters. Try some rub-on or glue-on commercial letters.
- (b) Have contrast between letters and background.
- (c) Incorporate commonly used and understandable words.
- (d) Keep the text current, geared for today.

(3) Shock Value.

    (a) Use unusual features, three dimensional materials, animation from battery operated motors, (donated from the supermarket), pastel chalk on dull paper, cartoons.

    (b) Letters cut from magazines, or even whole words, glued on. Animated letters:

Figure 19-1

    (c) Use of yarn, cloth, decorative paper, newpapers. Paint lettering on classified page of newspaper. Use pictures from greeting cards, stick figures, hand to point.

Figure 19-2

Construction:

Use sturdy cardboard or piece of corrigated carton for base.
"A" frame design or fold out support at back can both be stored flat to save space.

Materials:

Save from packing received at facility, art stores, donations, display supply houses. The latter is worth the trip to see new materials and get new ideas. Scotch and masking tape and glue can be used to assemble.

Where to display:

Indoor: Walls, bulletin boards, counters. Mobile type from ceiling (hard to read, put words on both sides.)

Outdoor: At entrance doors. (Older people tend to look straight ahead, at eye level, not very far up or down, so consider this when placing posters meant for them to read.)

NEWSLETTER

The newsletter of a facility is designed for people to read and enjoy, so it should be about people. It should include what is happening and what is planned for future enjoyment. Birthdays, new residents, activity calendars, religious services, and personality sketches will make good content. It is an absorbing project for residents, volunteers, or a combination of both, but it will take one person to guide it from start to finish. This is where the Activity Program Director comes in.

Format will be determined by the means of reproduction. We have found mimeograph to be most satisfactory. Length as well as colors can vary. Cartoons and illustrations, even photographs can be used in this printing method. We use a large print typewriter or all capitals to cut the stencils so that older eyes can more easily read the contents. The stencils and the typewriter which is used to cut them, hold the key to the success of the newsletter. So be sure the person doing this part knows his business. The operation of the mimeograph machine is easily done by the residents, also the stacking, stapling and folding of the finished product.

Ideas for content can come from other facilities' newsletters. The local Council on Aging, usually a Community Fund Agency, will publish a comprehensive monthly news-sheet, including the programs of all the senior citizen groups in the area. These will keep you abreast of what is going on with others in the same age bracket. So be sure you subscribe to all of them.

DISPLAYING OF PRODUCTS

A display area is necessary if the products, handwork and crafts made by the residents are to be sold. It is a good public relations effort to let others know what has been going on in the activity department and this sales program also keeps the enthusiasm high in the producers. Two or three wall shelves in a bright corner of the workroom will hold a variety of items. If you are lucky enough to have a glass display case, keep it attractively full. We prefer to have the finished product displayed in the work area where visitors can see the projects in the making and the eagerness of the workers.

Paintings, sketches and other types of flat art work can be displayed on walls. Why not have an area, somewhere in the facility, to hang a "Back Fence Art Show" continuously. The dining room, if there are good background walls, would be an excellent area for the enjoyment of the residents' efforts.

If you display your wares outside the facility, at a fair for instance, take a tip from the commercial display artists and use covered boxes to produce several levels and vertical surfaces for hanging some of the items.

Chapter 20

WHERE TO GO

FOR HELP

This chapter will be devoted to sources for additional help in developing activity programs for senior citizens. Books, pamphlets, and visual aids will be listed according to subject area. We urge you to be curious continually about new techniques, new products, new ideas and combinations of both new and old. There are always new developing sources to help you; be flexible in finding them.

WHERE TO BUY MATERIALS AND EQUIPMENT

Contact the central supply department for the facility. Through this department materials and equipment may be available at wholesale prices. They have numerous catalogues for locating materials.

Local dry goods and hardware stores will be receptive to your needs, provide information and advice about new products, and be of help, if you ask.

Specialty, gift, craft and hobby shops will be inspirational as well as serving as sources for supplies.

Use the yellow pages of your telephone book.

Request mail order catalogues from arts and crafts supply houses.

SOURCES OF PATTERNS AND IDEAS

After some experience, you will be able to develop patterns from pictures. At first, however, there are several good general sources for them.

Commercial patternmakers, usually available in department stores.
Magazines—Arts and crafts
                Womens and household
                Needlecraft
                Specialty
Newspaper syndicated articles
Public schools have arts and crafts curriculums which can be helpful
Encyclopedias
Library books
Hobby and craft stores
Attending exhibits and craft demonstrations

GENERAL SOURCES OF INFORMATION AND ADVICE

Visual Aids

Training
These training aids are usually available at some expenses.
Request current lists and regulations.

Pfizer Medical Film Library
    267 W. 25th St.
    New York, N.Y., 10001
Public Health Service Audio-Visual Facility
    Atlanta, Ga., 30333
American Foundation for the Blind
    15 W. 16th St.
    New York, N.Y., 10011
Smith, Kline and French Labs   (remotivation materials)
    1500 Spring Garden St.
    Philadelphia, Pa. 19101
American Hospital Association Film Library
    840 No. Lake Shore Dr.
    Chicago, Ill., 60611
State Health Departments-film library
State Universities & Land Grant Colleges—film libraries

Entertainment and *enjoyment.* (movies, films and slides). These films are usually free, if you pick them up, or available for the postage cost. Send for information on current films and arrangements.
Public and Private libraries. (city, county, state)
Museums
National airlines, local offices
Railroad lines

Foreign consuls & embassies
University and college libraries
Oil companies
Private and public utilities, power, telephone, water.
Films Inc. (subsidiary of Encyclopedia Britannica Films, Inc.)
   1150 Wilmette Ave.
   Wilmette, Illinois, 60091
Private film distributing cos.
Walt Disney Films
   5625 Hollywood Blvd.
   Hollywood, Cal., 90028
State game department
Local photographers and hobbyists
Families of residents who travel

Projectors and screens may be borrowed or rented from some libraries, schools, churches, and individuals. It may be a wise investment to have your own if you use them at least once a week.

BIBLIOGRAPHY

Section I

Organizations Providing Literature on the Subject of the Senior Citizen

American Association of Homes for the Aging
   315 Park Ave South
   New York, N.Y., 10010
American Heart Association   (strokes, C.V.A. & rehabilitation techniques)
   44 E. 23rd St.
   New York, N.Y., 10010
National Council on the Aging
   44 W. 45th St
   New York, N.Y., 10036
American Nursing Home Association   (official journal—*Nursing Homes*)
   1025 Connecticut Ave.
   Washington, D.C., 20201
National Council of Senior Citizens, Inc.
   1627 K St. N.W.
   Washington, D.C., 20006
National Easter Seal Society for Crippled Children and Adults (monthly publication—*Rehabilitation Literature* survey of National associations and their educational materials)

2023 W. Ogden Ave.

Chicago, Ill., 60612

American Medical Association, Committee on Aging

535 N. Dearborn St.

Chicago, Ill., 60610

How the Older Person Can Get the Most Out of Living and *a New Concept of Aging.*)

United States Dept. of Health, Education and Welfare

Washington, D.C., 20201

Rehabilitation Record—Social & Rehabilitation Service)

(*Aging*—Administration on Aging)

Faunce, Frances A., *The Nursing Home Visitor*, N.Y., Abingdon Press. 1969.

Bengson, Evelyn, O.T.R., *Guide to Planning and Equipping a Handicraft Facility for a Nursing Home Activity Program*, Washington State Dept. of Health, Olympia, Washington. $2. Published April 1964, 88 pages. Pay State Treasurer. The purpose of the guide is to give a nursing home administrator a brief, well-rounded awareness of what to consider in planning a handicraft program. It deals with space, equipment, attitudes and projects for the nursing home, and delves into the use of community groups to aid the program.

Local Medical Society Journals

Geriatric Institutions—National Geriatrics Society

11 E. 48th St.

New York, 10017

Geriatric Nursing and Professional Nursing Home—Miller Publishing Co.

2501 Wayzata Blvd.

Minneapolis, Minn., 55440

Nursing Homes—4015 West 65th St.

Minneapolis, Minn., 55435

Patient Care—Miller & Fink Publishing Corp.

165 West Putnam Ave.

Greenwich, Conn., 06830

Geriatrics—Lancet Publishing Co., Inc

4015 W. 65th St.

Minneapolis, Minn., 55435

Rehabilitation Literature—National Easter Seal Society

2023 West Ogden Ave.

Chicago, Ill., 60612

The Oldster—Wisconsin Dept. of Health and Social Services.

1 W. Wilson St.

Madison, Wisc., 53702

Accent on Living—802 Reinthaler
> Bloomington, Illinois, 61701

Journal of the American Geriatrics Society—Williams & Wilkins Co.
> Baltimore, Maryland, 21202

Modern Nursing Home—McGraw-Hill Pub.
> 1050 Merchandise Mart
> Chicago, Ill., 60654

Modern Maturity—American Association of Retired Persons
> 1225 Connecticut Ave. N.W.
> Washington, D.C., 20036

Social Work Training Manual for Nursing Home Personnel—Dr. Forest Brown

> State Dept. of Health
> 3400 No. Eastern
> Oklahoma City,
> Oklahoma, 73105

Bibliography—Volunteers—Chapter 7

Manual from American Nursing Home Association
> 1025 Connecticut Ave. N.W.
> Washington, D.C. 20036
> (This is available only if your facility is a member.)

Being a Trained Volunteer
> Oregon State Board of Health
> State Office Building
> 1400 S.W. 5th Ave.
> Portland, Oregon

Activities for the Aged and Infirm
> *Toni Merrill, M.A.*
> *Chas. C. Thomas, Pub.*

Recreational Activity Development for the Aging in Homes, Hospitals, and Nursing Homes
> Carol Lucas Ed. D.
> Charles C. Thomas, Pub.

Starting a Recreation Program in Institutions for the Ill or Handicapped Aged
> Morton Thompson Ed. D.
> National Recreation Association
> 8 West 8th St.
> New York, New York, 10011

A Program of Recreation for the Homebound Adult
> Morton Thompson Ed. D.
> National Recreation Association
> 8 West 8th St.
> New York, New York, 10011

Bibliography—Special Needs of Physically Handicapped—Chapter 8

Handbook For One-Handers—Aaron L. Danzig
    Federation of the Handicapped
    211 W. 14th St., New York, N.Y., 10011
Dysphasia—McKenzie Buck Ph.D
    Prentice-Hall, Inc., 1968
    Englewood Cliffs, N.J. 07632
Up & Around—Strike Back at Stroke
    U.S. Dept. of Health, Education & Welfare
    Public Health Service
    Division of Chronic Diseases
    Washington, D.C., 20201
Do It Yourself Again
    American Heart Association
    44 E. 23rd St., New York, N.Y., 10010
Rehabilitative Nursing Techniques 1,2,3 & 4
    American Rehabilitation Foundation
    1800 Chicago Ave., Minneapolis, Minn., 55404
Self-Help Devices for Rehabilitation
    New York University—Bellevue Medical Center
    Wm. C. Brown Co.
    Dubuque, Iowa
J. A. Preston Company, 175 5th Ave., New York, N.Y., 10003
Be O.K. Sales Company, Box 32, Brookfield, Ill., 60513
Homemaking for the Handicapped—May, Waggoner & Brettke. Dodd, Mead & Co., 1966
The Lamplighter (Mail Order House)
    10 W. Fordham Road, New York, N.Y., 10468
St. Otto's Song Books—"Let's Sing It Again" $1.25
    Transcript Pub. Co.
    Little Falls, Minn., 56345
Language Problems After a Stroke
    American Rehabilitation Foundation
    1800 Chicago Ave, Minneapolis, Minn., 55404

Addresses for Help with the Blind:

American Foundation for the Blind, Inc.
    15 W. 16th St., New York, N.Y., 10011
American Brotherhood for the Blind, Inc.
    P.O. Box 500, Nashua, New Hampshire
Association of Hospital & Institution Libraries
    50 E. Huron St. Chicago, Illinois
    (List of reading aids for the handicapped.)

Xerox Corporation
P.O. Box 24, Rochester, N.Y., 14601
(Large type books and periodicals)
New York Times
Times Square, N.Y., N.Y., 10036
(Large type weekly edition)
New England Council of Optometrists, Inc.
101 Tremont St., Boston, Mass.
National Aid to Visually Handicapped
3201 Balboa St., San Francisco, Calif., 94121

Additional Sources of Information

Garden, Warren H., Ph. D. *Left Handed Writing.* The Interstate, 19 No. Jackson St., Danville, Illinois.

Richardson, Nina K., *Type With One Hand.* South-Western Publishing Co., Cincinnati, Ohio.

Gartner, John. N., *Large Type Reading Materials for the Visually Handicapped.* New Outlook For the Blind, October 1968.

Wooldridge, Dean E., *The Machinery of the Brain.* McGraw-Hill Book Co., Inc., New York, N.Y.

Rehabilitation Gazette, Box 149, Chagrin Fall, Ohio, 44022. (Magazine for Quadriplegics.)

Fashion-Able, P.O. Box 23188, Ft. Lauderdale, Florida, 33307 (Fashions for the handicapped)

Shalik's Rehabilitation Aides, 5931 S. W. 8th St., Miami, Florida, 33144

Rosenberg, Charlot, *Simple Self-Help Devices to Make for the Handicapped.* Damon & Faye Printing Co., 1734 Wildwood Rd N.E., Atlanta, Ga., 30306

Items That May Be Purchased to Assist the Physically Handicapped to Become More Independent, Georgia Warm Springs Foundation, Warm Springs, Georgia.

Homemaking Aids for the Disabled

Assistive Devices for the Handicapped
American Rehabilitation Foundation
1800 Chicago Ave.
Minneapolis, Minn., 55404

Section II

Hall, Babette, *The Right Angles,* Ives Washburn, Inc., N.Y., 1965
(A good basic book on how to do successful publicity and avoid the wrong angle or none at all. Illustrations are especially vivid)

Levy, Harold, P. *Public Relations For Social Agencies.* Harper and Brothers Publishers, N.Y., 1956. (Handbook, indexed which will give you help in knowing how to go about raising funds, recruiting volunteers, winning community support for your efforts and program.)

Depew, Arthur M. *The Cokesbury Party Book.* Parthenon Press, Nashville, Tennessee. (52 parties, not devised especially for senior citizens, but very useful and adaptable ideas are presented.)

A Guide to Books on Recreation:
National Recreation & Park Assoc.
1700 Pennsylvania Ave.
Washington, D.C., 20006

The following is a list of many more books on recreation:

Merrill, Toni *Activities For the Aged And Infirm.* Charles C. Thomas, Springfield, Illinois, 1967.

Haun, Paul. *Recreation: A Medical Viewpoint.* Bureau of Publications, Teachers College, Columbia University, New York, 1965

Thompson, Morton. *A Program of Recreation for the Homebound Adult.* National Recreation & Park Assoc., 1700 Penn. Ave., Wash., D.C.

Thompson, Morton. *Starting a Recreation Program in Institutions for the Ill or Handicapped Aged,* National Recreation & Park Assoc., 1700 Penn. Ave., Washington, D.C., 20006

Masters, Peggy and Robert. *101 Best Stunts and Novelty Games.* Sterling Publications Co., Inc., New York.

Depew, Arthur M. *The Cokesbury Game Book.* The Parthenon Press, Nashville, Tenn., 1960

Bell, R.C. *Board and Table Games.* Oxford University Press, London, England, 1960

Ickis, Marguerite. *Pastimes for the Patient.* A.S. Barnes Co., Inc., New York

Bowen, Georgene E. *Merrily We Play.* Education-Recreation Division of the Health and Welfare Council, 1617 Pennsylvania Blvd., Philadelphia, Pennsylvania.

Chapman, Frederick, M. *Recreational Activities for the Handicapped.* Ronald Press Co., N.Y., 1960. (Has many easy games and suggestions for music.)

Eisenberg, Helen and Larry. *How to Help Folks Have Fun.* American Book, Stratford Press Inc., N.Y., 1954. (Excellent—hints of all types.)

Kaplan, Jerome. *A Social Program for Older People.* University of Minnesota Press, Minneapolis, 1953. (Information of centers, volunteers. How to get people to participate.)

Kubie, Susan H. *Group Work With Aged.* International University Press, Inc., N.Y., 1953. (Describes experiences in a center.)

Leonard, Charles. *Recreation Through Music.* A.S. Barnes and Co., N.Y., 1952. (Good guide in how to use music in programs.)

Lucas, Carol. *Recreational Activity Development for the Aging in Homes, Hospitals, and Nursing Homes.* Published by Charles C. Thomas, Springfield, Ill., 1962. (Interesting form sheets, certificates for volunteer service; general advice in how to build a program; extensive bibliography.)

National Recreation Association. *Recreational Activities for Adults.* Associated Press, N.Y., 1950. (Has many good suggestions for games.)

Ostrow, Alvert A. *Time Fillers.* Harper and Bros., N.Y., 1952. (Ideas of how to spend leisure time alone.)

Thompson, Nellie Zella. *High Times:* 700 Suggestions for Social Activities. E. P. Dutton and Co., Inc., 1950. (Geared for teenagers, but has many ideas, parties, decorating, etc.)

Wahlskow, Catherine Lee. *Add Life to Their Years.* Toledo Council of Social Welfare, 1952. Department of Publishing and Distribution, 120 E. 23rd Street, New York, N.Y. (Good reference material—$1.00)

Welfare and Health Council, New York City, 1955. $ .50. (Has an extensive bibliography on sources of material and leadership; program ideas and instructions.)

Williams, Arthur Milton. *Recreation in the Senior Years.* Associated Press, N.Y. Compiled for the National Recreation Association, 1962. (Good general reference)

Section III

General Craft Books

Turner, G. Alan, *Creative Crafts for Everyone.* The Viking Press, New York. 1959

Hils, Karl, *Creative Crafts,* Reinhold Publishing Corp., Inc., New York.

Ickis, Marguerite & Reba S. Esh *The Book of Arts and Crafts.* Dover Publications, Inc., New York, 1954.

Ickis, Marguerite. *Pastimes for the Patient.* A.S. Barnes & Co., Inc., New York, 1966.

Johnson, Pauline. *Creating with Paper.* University of Washington Press, Seattle, Washington, 1958.

Taubes, Frederic. *The Quickest Way to Draw Well.* The Studio Publications, Inc., in association with Thomas Y. Crowell Co., New York and London. 1958.

Wolchonok, Louis. *Design for Artists and Craftsmen.* Dover Publications, Inc., New York, 1953

At Your Fingertips—Complied by the Colorado Occupational Therapy Association, Denver, Colorado. Smith Brooks Printing Co., 1954.

Boehm, Peggy. *Knitting Without Needles.* Sterling Publishing Co., Inc., New York, 1965.

Johnston, Meda Parker & Glen Kaufman. *Design On Fabrics.* Reinhold Publishing Corp., New York, 1967.

Weisinger, Mort. *1001 Valuable Things You Can Get Free.* Bantam Paper Back Books Inc., New York, 10016. 1968.

Crafts for the Aging and Crafts for Retirement. published by: American Craftsman's Council, 29 W. 53rd St., New York, 10019

Magazines and Pamphlets

Nutmeg House Crafts. Joy Road Studio, 48234 Joy Road, Plymouth, Michigan. 48170

The Idea Exchange. Occupational Therapy Dept., Kalamazoo State Hospital, Kalamazoo, Michigan, 49001

School Arts Magazine. Printer's Building, Worcester, Mass.

Catalogues

American Handicrafts Co.
2849 White Settlement Rd.
Ft. Worth, Texas

Wyco Products
814 Greenwood Ave.
Jenkintown, Pa., 19046

Magnus Craft Materials Inc.
108 Franklin St.
New York, 10013

Griffin Craft Supplies
P.O. Box 506
Oakland, Cal., 94604

S & S Arts and Crafts
Colchester, Conn., 06415

Dennison Manufacturing Co.,
Framingham, Mass., 10701

The Unicorn Catalogue. Books for Craftsmen.
Box 645
Rockville, Maryland, 20851

The Lily Mills Co.
Shelby, No. Carolina.

O-P Craft Co.,
Sandusky, Ohio, 44870

J.L. Hammett Co.,
Cambridge, Mass.

Ceramics

Reed, Carl & Joseph Orze, *Art From Scrap.* Worcester, Mass., Davis Publications, Inc., 1960.

Lavoos, Janice & Felice Paramore. *Modern Mosiac Techniques.* New York, N.Y., Watson-Guptill Publishers, 1960.

Hofsted, Jolyon. *Step By Step Ceramics.* Wayne Warehouse Corp., 150 Parish Dr., Wayne, New Jersey, 074706.

Kenny, John B. *The Complete Book of Pottery Making.* Stewart Clay Co., New York., 1959.

Modeling With Clays. American Art Clay Co., Indianapolis, Indiana.

Sewing

Carroll, Alice. *The Goodhousekeeping's Complete Book of Needlecraft.* New York, Doubleday. 1947.

Enthoven, Jacqueline. *Stitchery For Children.* New York, Reinhold Corp. 1969.

King, Bucky. *Creative Canvas Embroidery.* New York, Hearthside Press, 1963.

Thomas, Mary. *Embroidery Book.* New York, William Morrow & Co.

Krevitsky, Nick. *Stitchery.* New York, Reinhold Publishing Co.

Weaving

Atwater, Mary M. *Shuttle-Craft Book of American Handweaving.* New York, Macmillan Co. 1944.

Wilson, Jean. *Weaving Is for Everyone.* New York, Reinhold Publishing Corp. 1967.

Ramey, Sarita. *Weaving Without a Loom.* Worcester, Mass., Davis Publications. 1966.

Thorpe, Azalea S. & Jack L. Larsen. *Elements of Weaving.* Garden City, New York, Doubleday & Co. 1967.

Additional Catalogues

The Handcrafters, Waupun, Wisconsin.

Bergman Looms, Rt. I, Box 185, Poulsbo, Washington, 98370.

Waste Materials

Reed, Carl & Joseph Orze. *Art From Scrap.* Worcester, Mass., Davis Publications, Inc. 1960.

Pack-O-Fun Magazine. 14 Main St., Park Ridge, Illinois, 60068.

Lukowitz, Joseph J. *55 New Tin-Can Projects.* Milwaukee, Wisconsin, The Bruce Publishing Co., 1954.

Howard, Sylvia W. *Tin-Can Crafting.* New York, Sterling Publishing Co. Inc.

Men's Projects

Harvey, Virginia. *Macrame.* New York, Reinhold Publishing Corp. 1967.

Origami. Japanese Publications Trading Co., P.O. Box 469, Rutland, Vermont.

Aller, Doris. *Sunset Woodcarving Book.* Menlo Park, Cal., Lane Publishing Co.

Delta Craft Books, Rockwell Mfg. Co., Pittsburgh, Pa., 1954.

And last, not least in each perplexing case
Learn the sweet magic of a cheerful face,
Not always smiling, but at least serene,
When grief and anguish crowd the anxious scene.
Each look, each movement, every word and tone
Should tell the patient you are all his own.
Not the mere artist, purchased to attend
But the warm, ready, self-forgetting friend
Whose genial presence in itself combines
The best of cordials, tonics, anodynes.

Oliver Wendell Holmes 1849

Index

INVENTORY 74

FALL 77

INVENTORY 1983